Greater Things Generation: 8 Ways to Walk in the Supernatural

By Tara Essman

All Bible verses referred to and quoted in this book are from the New International Version.

INTRODUCTION

A few years ago, I was challenged with the truth of scripture which obliterated my preconceived ideas and theology about healing, miracles, and the supernatural. From that time on, I have never been the same. God has challenged my faith in ways I could never have dreamed. He has called me out of the boat and into the waves. I am driven to pursue this realm of the impossible. The desire in me to see people completely healed, delivered, and restored has driven me to pursue more and more of Jesus. I want to know Him- all of Him. It is the desire of my heart that not only I would know Him, but to help others discover the fullness of Jesus Christ as well, not just a watered-down churchy version of Him.

I am not satisfied to just read about Jesus. Anything less than the New Testament and New Church experiences that I read about in the Word of God will do. I want to experience what the woman with the issue of blood experienced. A touch- and she was instantly healed! This woman has taught me more about faith than anyone else. I want what the disciples experienced when they went out two by two and saw signs and wonders. I want these "greater things" that Jesus spoke about in **John 14:12**. I want what all the great faith healers from the past had, and the common denominator they shared is that they all believed that it was Jesus' will to heal, and that He paid the price for it, and guess what? They saw results. They walked in the miraculous. Do you want results? Do you want to walk in the miraculous? I do. I want Jesus! That is my heart, and this is my pursuit- to continue knocking on the door of healing. The door has been cracked open but I know as keep knocking the door will be opened wider and wider.

I have discovered that the topic of healing is just as controversial as religion in general or even politics. I have met people who want to argue whatever reason they can think of to explain why Jesus does not heal, or why He allows certain sicknesses or diseases, or that it is His will that we are sick. There have been tears over this subject when I have taught it. Isn't that crazy? I have learned that some people want to hold on to their skewed theology that Jesus wants us to be sick and that it is HIS will to allow sickness to make us better people. They exalt their own ideas, and their own beliefs, and what they have been taught over the truth of the Word. I used to be one of those people. Not anymore. I know that many will disagree with what I have to say, and there will be many opinions, reasons, and even scriptures to back up why I am wrong on this subject of healing, but that is ok. It will not stop me. I am driven by the words of Jesus when he said, "these signs shall accompany those who believe," in **Mark 16:17**.

If you are believer in Jesus, then you are qualified to walk in the supernatural. That is all there is to it. There are no other qualifications. So, how come more believers are not seeing these signs wonders, and miracles that we read about in the Bible? These are all questions I intend to address in this book. I have had to learn to pursue God no matter what obstacle is in my way. I will not allow the theology, doctrine, opinions, or-the persuasion of others to deter me from my quest of going after all that God has purchased for His children. If He died to give it to me, then it is worth having. There are levels of revelation, and He has more for those who will seek more.

The Lord has taken me on an Interesting journey. It is MY journey, and this is why I am writing. I want to share with you my discoveries because I believe that my experiences can help others. I am not satisfied until I see the church walking in the fullness of Christ.

Bill Johnson says in *When Heaven Invades Earth*, "It is abnormal for a Christian NOT to have an appetite for the impossible. It has been written into our spiritual DNA to hunger for the impossibilities around us to bow at the name of Jesus." This sums up my heart. I truly am driven to pursue these impossibilities. Now, I have a voracious appetite for the impossible, where before, I was content and satisfied in my lack of witnessing any healings or being part of any. No more, If you are believer in Jesus Christ, then you are called to walk in the supernatural. Healing is for you, and you are called to operate in bringing healing to others. Jesus said in **John 14:12**, "... whoever believes in me will do the works I have been doing, and they will do even greater things than these..."

I am writing to the born- again Christian who is hungry for more of God. If you have an interest in the supernatural, or if you want to learn more about it, or you want to learn how to walk in the supernatural then this book is for you. Maybe you have always wondered what it would take to see the miraculous in your own life. You are about to find out. If for some reason you are not a born again believer in Jesus Christ I would be amiss if I did not caution you. An interest in the supernatural apart from God is very dangerous. God is good. He loves you, and He created you with purpose. To become a believer is very simple. All you have to do is ask Jesus into your heart. Ask Him to forgive you of your sins, and ask Him to help you follow Him all the days of your life. If you do that, and if you are sincere, then that means you are saved, born again, a believer, a saint, a follower of Jesus. I encourage you to find a church home where you can grow and be discipled as a new believer. You were bought at a price. You are not your own. Offer yourself as a living sacrifice to God and He will use you in amazing ways to bring life and hope to others in this dark world. You are the Greater Things Generation that the title of this book speaks of. You would not be reading this book if you were not hungry for more of God. Walking in the supernatural should be a part of your everyday life. Are you ready?

It's time for the church to walk in what was declared and promised by Jesus. Jesus is waiting for your action to come in alignment with your faith. It's not rocket

science. Let's take this journey together to become a "greater things generation." I have learned through experience that these eight things can help every believer learn to operate in the supernatural to bring healing to the sick.

CHAPTER 1: PURSUE INTIMACY

Developing a life in God's presence above all else is the only way to fulfill our God-given destinies. Keys to our callings are released when we spend time there. — Heidi Baker -Birthing the Miraculous: The Power of Personal Encounters with God to Change Your Life and the World

The day our first child was born forever changed my life. It was in April of 1995 that my husband and I first held her in our arms and looked at her precious little face. I was overcome by a love so overwhelming that it is hard to explain or understand unless you are a mother. I knew that I treasured her, and how deeply I loved her. She was Just a baby- a helpless, precious, tiny, little thing who needed to be loved, nurtured, and cared for so she could thrive and grow to be healthy in every way. As her mother I knew how committed I was to her, to be there for her, no matter what. Our relationship naturally grew over the years as we lived life spending time together with each other and with our family. I learned what was important to her, what she liked, and what she did not like. Those early years were the easy ones. It was the preteen and teen years where it started to get challenging , but it was during these times that she learned that she would always hear the truth from her Dad and I. She knew that we loved her unconditionally.

Life was not always perfect, nor was our relationship, but we did learn how to communicate effectively with each other. We learned about each other as we lived life togehter...as we spent time together. She is now a healthy twenty-three year old at the writing of this book, and we have a close affectionate relationship. It took daily devotion, commitment, and work to develop our relationship.

Dictionary.com defines intimacy as "a close, familiar, and usually affectionate or loving personal relationship with another person or group; close association with or a detailed knowledge or deep understanding of a place, subject."

All relationships require some level of intimacy to be healthy. Relationships without intimacy are cold and lifeless. That is not the kind of relationship God wants to have with His children. He wants to have an affectionate, loving, and personal relationship with each of us. God desires that we would know Him with deep understanding and with detailed knowledge. The only way that is possible is to develop an intimate relationship with our Creator.

God Designed Us to Desire Intimacy

God designed humanity to desire intimacy. Why? Because we are made in the image of God. He desires intimacy, therefore, so do we because we are a reflection of Him. Adam and Eve had an intimacy with God that provokes me to jealousy. They walked with God in the cool of the day. Adam and Eve in the Garden of Eden is the model for how God has always wanted to relate to His creation. From the very beginning God desired intimacy with us. That is the desire of His heart- for us to choose Him, to fellowship with Him, and to commune with Him. He does not want to force us to be with Him, nor does He want us to want Him ONLY when we want something. Just like a parent would be hurt if their children only wanted to be nice to them when they wanted something,

God feels the same way. He does not want us to seek Him only when our motives are selfish. That is immature love. That is what small children do. They beg for candy, they cry for a soda, or for a new toy. It is a parent's joy when their child matures and enjoys being with them. God is delighted when we willingly choose to be WITH him, to want Him, to be intimate with Him. It shows a level of maturity when we grow in depth in our relationship with our Heavenly Father.

Randy Clark, a veteran healer of today says, "Anyone who does not have an experience with God, does not know God." I wholeheartedly agree. Why would he say that? Because God is a person to be known. He is not an abstract idea or a concept. He is a person. This is the most fundamental thing I have learned in my walk with Jesus. Intimacy with my God changed my life.

Fruit Flows From Intimacy

I want to make thing one clear though. As a believer, especially as a believer who is seeking the supernatural, sometimes our quest becomes too much on pursuing miracles, signs, and wonders, and not enough on pursuing God, the Miracle Maker. God desires that we would seek Him. As we seek Him, and are intimate with Him, the power will follow. Fruit flows from intimacy. Something gets birthed in the secret place with God. As I have pursued Him, it is amazing how the supernatural has increased in my own life. I have never been as close to God as I am now, but I do not intend to stay there. I intend to grow closer and closer to Him every day. I know I will never arrive spiritually, and that I should never park or camp out thinking I have attained some secret spiritual knowledge. I should keep pursuing and going after God. We should always continue to grow in God. Never let the enemy lie to you and tell you that you have learned all you need to learn. Since I have learned and am still learning this "intimacy thing," I hear God's heart like never before. I see people in a new light. I see them as He sees them, and often God gives me glimpses of His heart for them.] pray for more people than I ever have, and I have seen results. Let me share one example. This past year, I heard a friend of mine who I work with, complain of leg pain. I did not want her to be in pain, so without even thinking about what I was doing, I immediately laid my hand on her leg and said, "Be healed in Jesus' Name." She said, "Thank you," and that was it. I went on about my day and she went on about hers. Later on in the day, she came up to me and said, "When you prayed for my leg, I felt a heat, and then a little bit later, I noticed that the pain was completely gone." Isn't that awesome? We were not in church. I did not pray a long drawn out prayer. God honored my very simple prayer of faith for her to be healed.

I share that with you to say that I never would have done that before. But as I have grown in my relationship with Jesus and have learned to be intimate with Him, I have a desire to pray for people. My heart goes out to them because I do not want them to suffer or to be in pain. Just as I shared how my daughter feels safe to share things with me, in the Presence of God, I feel safe to do things that I would never have done before.

Jesus Withdrew to Pray

The Bible tells us that Jesus often went to solitary places to pray- to recharge. He was constantly surrounded by crowds. People wanted a piece of him. He withdrew from the crowds to have alone time with His Father. It was in these private times with His Father that Jesus was renewed, and reminded of His mission. It kept Him focused and on course. It is crucial in our relationship with our Heavenly Father that you and I do the same. Without intimacy, all that is left is religion. That was me for years in my personal walk. I lacked intimacy so all I had was religion. I had church, I had Bible study, but I had a pathetic prayer life. I believed the Bible, but my lack of intimacy with the Father caused me to be dry spiritually. I had a belief with no results. I was a leader in my church, I taught weekly, and even preached on occasion, but I saw no healings, had no words of knowledge, and unfortunately I could be legalistic, too. I was so dissatisfied when it came to church, my relationship with God, and with the things of the Spirit that I was desperate for something more, but I did not know what it was. Something deep inside of me was crying out for more. It was in my pursuit of more I discovered my Daddy God. How did I discover Him? Intimacy. This forever changed me. I learned about soaking in His presence. I learned that being with Him changed my perspective on things. I learned how to hang out with God. I am still learning, but I can promise you that being intimate with God is so much better than dry church. It was in these times of intimacy with God that He spoke new things to me. He shared His heart with me. He inspired

me. He encouraged me. I also learned to share my heart with Him. I made a new discovery. He was my "Eureka". As a matter of fact, the Lord spoke that word to me over four years ago, and it was not until recently that I understood it completely. Discovering Jesus in this whole new way was my "Eureka", my discovery - my aha moment! Jesus is my well that never runs dry. He is the Living Water I need to live in this world and to do life. It is that Living Water that I bring into every situation when I pray.

The Fruit from a Lack of Intimacy is Lack

I want to look at the lives of the Pharisees to demonstrate this point. The Pharisees pursued service to God. They obeyed the law, but most of them missed God's heart. Why did Jesus call them "white washed tombs full of dead men's bones" in **Matthew 23:27**? Because they looked good on the outside, and they said and did all the right things, but their hearts were dead. They had cerebral knowledge of God, but that was the extent of it. They elevated tradition over a relationship with God, and that kept them from hearing and seeing the truth when TRUTH was right in front of them. In Mark 7:6-8, He replied, "Isaiah was right when he prophesied about you hypocrites; as it is written: "These people honor me with their lips, but their hearts are far from me. 7 They worship me in vain;their teachings are merely human rules.'!! 8 You have let go of the commands of God and are holding on to human traditions."

Jesus would often say, "He who has ears, let them hear." **Matthew 11:15**. The spiritual ear of the Pharisee, in general, was deaf. Why were their spiritual ears deaf? Because they lacked intimacy. Intimacy revives the heart! Some of you need a resurrection of your heart. In **2Corinthians 3:6** Paul writes, "it is the law that kills, but the Spirit gives life!" The Pharisees lived by the letter of the law, but the law pointed to Christ. He was the fulfillment of the law, but they missed that. The law was never the answer. Jesus was, yet they were clueless! God was in the flesh, right in front of them, and they never had an inkling that it was Him.

Fruit comes from intimacy. What kind of fruit did the Pharisees have? None! Zilch! Jesus told them they were the blind leading the blind. In other words, He was telling them that they themselves were blind to the truth, yet they attempted to teach and lead those that looked up to them and saw them as having all the answers. They had the law, but they did not let the law or the Word lead them to Jesus. In **Mark 11:12-14** it says, "The next day as they were leaving Bethany, Jesus was hungry. '? Seeing in the distance a fig tree in leaf, he went to find out if it had any fruit. When he reached it, he found nothing but leaves, because it was not the season for figs. '4 Then he said to the tree, "May no one ever eat fruit from you again." And his disciples heard him say it."

This is the only destructive miracle Jesus did. Why did he do that? Even though the fig tree was not in season, it should have had some unripe green figs on it. It did not. It was just taking up space in the ground. It was not producing life. God often used the fig tree as a metaphor for the nation of Israel when it came to judgment. The tree had leaves on it, and it was blooming, but it had no fruit, not even a hint of one, so Jesus cursed it. The Pharisees were like that fig tree. They had green leaves and they looked good, but they produced NO fruit, NO life. Instead, of helping others and leading them to God, they oppressed people. **Matthew 23:13-17** says, "Woe to you, teachers of the law and Pharisees, you hypocrites! You shut the door of the kingdom of heaven in People's faces. You yourselves do not enter, nor will you let those enter who are trying to. Woe to you, teachers of the law and Pharisees, you hypocrites! You travel over land and sea to win a single convert, and when you have succeeded, you make them twice as much a child of hell as you are "Woe to you, blind guides! You say, 'If anyone swears by the temple, it means nothing; but anyone who swears by the gold of the temple is bound by that oath.' " You blind fools! Which is greater: the gold, or the temple that makes the gold sacred?"

Jesus saw straight to their hearts. They did not allow the very truths they studied and could recite from memory to penetrate their own hearts. Instead, they put such strict regulations on people that were impossible to fulfill. All of the traditions they created caused people to feel inadequate and oppressed. Jesus told them they shut the door of the Kingdom of heaven in people's faces, and they could not enter themselves, but they keep the ones who do want to enter from entering. The saddest part is that they thought they were righteous and they thought they were pleasing God, but God was standing right in front of them, yet they never knew it.

The Pharisees, in general, hindered the work of the Kingdom. Their lack of understanding and lack of revelation of the heart of God was the problem. Their lack of intimacy with God led to their own puffed up ideologies of themselves and they were a stumbling block to others. The Pharisees should have been leading people to a genuine encounter with God, but they did the exact opposite. As believers we are to point people to Jesus. I don't know about you, but I do not ever want to hinder the work of the Kingdom. I do not want to be a stumbling block to others. I want to point others to Jesus Christ and His marvelous Kingdom.

A Lack of Intimacy Breeds Legalism

Also, a lack of intimacy may often cause people to be legalistic and then they mistakenly call it religion. You have seen examples of this. Like when people hold up signs that say, "God hates fags," and they do it in the name of Christianity. People often think they are doing God a favor with their harsh actions towards sin or with what they think is a defense of the Gospel. That is what the Apostle Paul did before he became a Christian. He really thought he was right when he was murdering Christians. He thought he was righteous and that he was doing God a favor. It was not until he had an encounter with Jesus that he saw how wrong he had been. It was revelation that changed Paul's heart. Up until then, Paul was the Pharisee of all Pharisees.

Recently, the Supreme Court ruled in favor of gay marriage in all 50 states. The posts seen on social media grieve my heart. People can be vicious. I am not surprised when lost people act like lost people. Why? Because they are lost. Their minds and hearts are not renewed therefore they follow after their flesh, but what does surprise me is the behavior of so-called Christians, however, I do understand that it is a lack of intimacy with God that is at the root of such behavior. Without intimacy we exalt religion and legalism over people. I know that these people know the Word of God. They are speaking truth, but we are called to speak truth in love. Bashing people with scripture will not change anyone's heart. It is godly sorrow that leads to repentance. Intimacy with God is the key because then we understand His heart for people. He teaches us to supernaturally love people where they are.

God loves people! He wants us to value each person just as He does. God does not delight in the death of the wicked. It is impossible to really value people and love them without loving God first. When we get to a place of true intimacy with God, we learn His heart. He gladly shows us His heart, and that changes ours. He wants to help people overcome their struggle. He does not want us to dominate them or bully them or make them feel small. The enemy will use a lack of intimacy to distort and pervert the truth of scripture where Christians are more legalistic than loving. This is exactly what the Pharisees did. Do not be like them. Instead of reading the scriptures to gain only head knowledge we should read the Word asking God to show us His heart. Experiencing the heart of God forever changes ours.

Jesus is our Model

Let's look at some things Jesus said and did that demonstrate the importance of pursuing intimacy. In Matthew 17, a man came to Jesus and asked him to deliver his son who was suffering from seizures caused by a demonic spirit. He told Jesus that he had brought his son to Jesus' disciples, but they could not heal him. Jesus delivered the boy, and later his disciples asked him how come they could not drive out the demon. One of Jesus' responses was, "these come out only through prayer and fasting" (Mark 9:9).

When you read the story closely, you will see that Jesus immediately delivered the boy. He did not pray and he did not fast, so why did he say that to his disciples if he did not pray or fast?

This is a lesson in intimacy. Jesus habitually prayed. It was part of His life to seek solitary places to pray. In **Luke 5:16** it says, "But Jesus often withdrew to lonely places and prayed..." It was out of these prayer times that Jesus grew spiritually stronger so that when He

encountered darkness, He had a deep well to draw from. He was full of the presence of God. When we dwell in the secret place of the Almighty, we abide in His shadow. An exchange happens. The more time we spend with Him, the more His shadow or His presence rests on us. **Psalm 91:1**, says,"Whoever dwells in the shelter of the Most High will rest in the shadow of the Almighty." We carry His Presence wherever we go and we release His Presence that was poured into us during those intimate times. Jesus modeled intimacy for us. We must cultivate and nurture our relationship with our Heavenly Father. We are called to seek Him first! Everything else will follow if we will just seek Him.

"Seek first His Kingdom and His righteousness and all of these things will be given to you as well" — **Matthew 6:33**. When Jesus was face to face with the demonic spirit he dealt with the situation and it was from the overflow of the time spent with His Father that enabled him to cast it out without prayer or fasting. These intimate times with God are vital for every believer. Jesus said some amazing things that give us some insight to His relationship with His Father.

John 6:16 -My teaching isn't mine, but is from the One who sent me.

John 8:26- What I have heard from Him, these things I tell the world.

John 8:38 -I speak what I have seen in the presence of the Father.

Intimacy Births Identity

Jesus knew who He was. He knew His mission. He knew that to accomplish His mission, He had to stay connected to the Father. We need to know who we are. We can no longer walk around in identity crisis. When we know our identity in Christ, we will understand our mission. To complete and fulfill our mission, we must stay connected to the Father. In **Matthew 16:13-20** Jesus asks his disciples who people say He is. The disciples' reply that they say He is John the Baptist, Elijah, Jeremiah, or one of the prophets. Then Jesus targets their hearts and asks them, "But what about you? Who do you say I am?" Simon Peter answered, "You are the Christ, the Son of the living God." Jesus replied, "Blessed are you Simon, son of Jonah, for this was not revealed to you by man, but by my Father in heaven. And I tell you that you are Peter, and on this rock I will build my church, and the gates of Hades will not overcome it. I will give you the keys of the kingdom of heaven; whatever you bind on earth will be bound in heaven and whatever you loose on earth will be loosed in heaven."

Peter's answer to Jesus' question was given to him through divine revelation. Jesus was saying to Peter, (my paraphrase) "because you know who I am, let me tell you who you are. You are no longer Peter, a shaking reed, but you are now a rock!" When we know who He is then we know who we are. Intimacy with our Heavenly Father gives us divine revelation into our own identity.

Jesus told us that we need to stay connected to Him in **John 15:15**, "I am the vine, and you are the branches. He who abides in me, will bear much fruit." I love this verse because right there Jesus promises results. "You will bear much fruit." If we abide or dwell with Him, we will bear much fruit. Just as Jesus dwelled with His Father, and spoke only what He heard His Father say, and did only what He saw His Father do, so must we. We must abide in Jesus. This is the key. Everything else will flow as we abide in Him.

Another thing we can learn from that same passage of scripture in **John 15** is that we can grow in intimacy. Jesus says, "I no longer call you servants, because a servant does not know his master's business. Instead, I have called you friends, for everything that I learned from my Father I have made known to you. ' You did not choose me, but I chose you and appointed you so that you might go and bear fruit—fruit that will last—and so that whatever you ask in my name the Father will give you. " This is my command: Love each other." **John 15:15-17**. This clearly shows levels of growth in our intimacy with Jesus. You can choose to remain a servant, or you can grow closer to Jesus in your relationship and become His friend. The choice is yours.

Moses was called a friend of God. True friends know your heart. Intimacy with the Father is the key that unlocks the mysteries of God and that will lead us to more and more revelation of Jesus Christ, and knowing that helps us understand who we are in Him. When we truly
discover our God-given identity, it changes the way we view the world, and that will change the way we pray.

Come Aside

Let's look at **Exodus 3** for a moment. "Now Moses was tending the flock of Jethro his father-in-law, the priest of Midian, and he led the flock to the far side of the wilderness and came to Horeb, the mountain of God. There the angel of the Lord appeared to him in the flames of fire from within a bush. Moses saw that though the bush was on fire, it did not burn up, so Moses thought, "I will go over and see this strange sight-why the bush does not burn up." When the Lord saw that he had gone over to look, God called to him from within the bush, "Moses, Moses!" God wanted to get Moses' attention so He did something supernatural. God was waiting for Moses to notice that the bush was not being consumed, and when he did, it was in Moses' "going over to look" that God spoke to him. God is waiting for us to come aside. God is waiting for us to notice Him. He wants us to pay attention to Him. It is in these moments of "coming aside" or "going over to look" that God speaks to us.

Grow On Purpose by Making Intimacy a Priority

How Do You Grow in Intimacy with God? That's a great question. I am glad you asked. It really is very simple.

1. You must do it on purpose. Jesus withdrew. He hung out with his disciples. He ministered to people. He had earthly relationships, but it was a priority of His to withdraw so that He could be alone with His Father. You must do the same. Find a place that you can get alone with God. It may be in your car. It may in your bedroom, or at the kitchen table at 5am when everyone else is asleep, but you must make it a priority. I have always tried to keep this very simple. I am married and have three children. My life can be extremely hectic, so I have not put extra pressure on myself. I know that life happens, but I do make time to get alone with God. My favorite place to pray is in my car. I have the best alone times with God in my car. I don't know where the most comfortable place for you will be, but you will discover it very soon. Do it on purpose! If you do not, you will not do it at all. If the enemy can

keep you from connecting with God then He has you right where he wants you.

2. Set aside a certain amount of time. Start somewhere. Start by maybe setting aside five minutes, and then grow from there. It is okay to start small. Do not despise small beginnings. Just like we steward or manage our finances, we must also steward our prayer life. It is something you can grow in. I started out with five or ten minutes and worked my way up. I can now pray up to two hours and now two hours feels like ten minutes. That did not happen overnight. I am not trying to sound overly spiritual here. I do not always pray for two hours, but sometimes I do, and when I do, I really enjoy

those times with my Father. Before, prayer was a chore. I could not focus. All I could think about was when I could stop. It is easy for me now when before it was not. You will find the same to be true for you. You will grow in this, so do not become discouraged. Hang in there and keep doing it.

3. You have to practice it. We have to practice His presence. Brother Lawrence, a 17th Century Carmelite Monk said this, "We have to learn to practice His presence." Still your life. Calm your spirit. Be still and know that He is God. In my opinion, it should not always look the same. We do not have to become legalistic in this. Be free. Sometimes it is appropriate to just sit or lay in His presence. Other times you may stand or walk in His presence. Sometimes there will be no talking on your part. Just hang out with Him and focus your heart on Him. Other times, it may be that you are praying and pouring out your heart to Him. There is no right way. Just seek Him. Make it a priority, and you will be amazed at what happens in your life. Develop your prayer life. You may like worship music on while you pray, or you may like it quiet. I do both. Sometimes the Lord tells me not to put on any music because He does not want any distractions during our time together, while other times I have the time of my life listening to

worship music. Ask the Holy Spirit to show you what to do. And if you still are not sure, then do what is comfortable for you, and you will begin to feel His presence and He will lead you and show you what to do. We must practice His presence. To develop a relationship with someone we have to spend time with them and get to know them.

I want to end this chapter with this quote by John Wimber. "The ability to hear what God is saying, to see what God is doing, and to move in the realm of the miraculous comes as an individual develops the same intimacy and dependence upon the Father as Jesus did. How did Jesus do what He did? The answer is found in His relationship with the Father. How will we do the "greater works than these," that Jesus promised? By discovering the same relationship of intimacy, simplicity, and obedience." —

CHAPTER 2: QUIT MAKING EXCUSES

"God always was the Healer. He is the Healer still...healing is for you. He never turned anyone away." ~ John G. Lake

Excuses Steal Our Purpose

Excuses! Ugh! They are ugly. We do not like it when we have been the recipient of someone else's excuse, but we must admit that we have all been guilty of creating our own excuses at one time or another. Excuses are a thief. They steal our purpose. The author of the excuse is the enemy. Excuses keep us inactive and ineffective. Satan loves to keep us ineffective in the Kingdom. If he can do that, then he has accomplished his purpose which is to keep Christians doing NOTHING. He does not have to get Christians to backslide, to fall back into sin like addiction, sexual promiscuity, etc. All he has to do is to keep us powerless, and excuses do exactly that.

I was the best excuse maker ever. I gave every reason I could think of to explain why God healed at times, but not in others. I made excuses about why I could not lay hands on the sick and see them healed. I disqualified myself. God never had to disqualify me. He did not have to. I did a good enough job of that all by myself. For years, I prayed generalized prayers for healing because that is all I knew to do. I mimicked the prayers of others. I did not know any better. I did not believe I was qualified in any way to lay hands on the sick or to pray for them. When someone whould ask me to pray, I prayed pathetic prayers that lacked faith like, "If it is your will, God, heal so and so," or "Be with the doctors and nurses as they perform surgery on so and so." I thought that laying hands on the sick was a job for the pastor or for the special evangelist or missionary that would come in and tell stories about their time on the mission field. I really did not believe it was something I could do. Then when I got the courage to actually lay hands on people to pray for their healing, I never saw anyone get healed. So, I rationalized why God did not heal them by saying things like, "He must want to heal you yet," or "He is making you a better person." I said those things to make myself more comfortable. I felt like I had to make up reasons as to why God was not healing them. I guess I felt like I had to make excuses for God. I had heard others do the same thing, so I not only made excuses for myself, but I also made excuses for God.

You want to know something? God does not need our excuses. He is God, and we are not. He showed us what to do. He told us what to do. So, what is the problem? Us! WE are the problem. Our own excuses trip us up. We must learn to get out of our own way and God's way. We need to quit making excuses for ourselves and for God. God created us with purpose and for purpose, but excuses keep us from fulfilling our purpose. The more we make excuses, the more time we waste accomplishing absolutely nothing!

We Must Take Action

As a believer it is imperative that we take the Word of God at face value. We cannot just believe what it says; we need to DO what the Word of God commands us to do. We have all made excuses. We all have had our reasons to justify why we did not do what we should have, but when it comes to healing, there are numerous excuses that keep us from stepping out in faith and doing what Jesus commanded us to do. In **Matthew 10:8**, Jesus says, "Heal the sick, raise the dead, cleanse those who have leprosy. Drive out demons. Freely you have received; freely give." That is our command. Obey-

ing a command requires action. Jesus told us what actions to do. Heal! Raise! Cleanse! Drive! Those are the action verbs. What excuses are keeping you from stepping out and doing what Jesus commanded? Let's look at some common excuses.

1. Fear- I'm scared to pray. What if nothing happens?

The number one reason is fear. Fear is debilitating. What if I pray and nothing happens? Here is a better question to ask yourself. What if something does happen? If you do pray and something happens, who would you give all of the glory to? Jesus, right? So, if you pray and nothing happens, are you supposed to carry that burden? No. Fear of praying and nothing happening is often the reason that we do not lay hands on the sick and pray for them. We have to push past fear and step into obedience. Fear keeps The Church crippled. If the enemy can make the church ineffective in the Kingdom, then he is gaining ground. By giving into fear we are making way for darkness to increase. God has called His children to bring increase to the earth, to pray "on earth as it is in heaven," but if we are only sitting in church pews, and playing church, and believing that people can be healed, but doing nothing to pursue it because of fear, then the Kingdom of God will not be advanced.

2. Looking foolish- What if I look foolish?

We often fear looking foolish. We have to get over that. This means that we are more concerned with the opinion of man rather than God. The fear of looking like an idiot if we pray for someone believing they will be healed but then they are not holds many back. Look at it this way, If you lay hands on someone, and believe that they can be healed, and you pray a prayer in faith, trusting God to bring about their healing, then you have done all that you can do. You must quit worrying about what others will think of you. It is this concern that keeps so many believers on the sidelines. God wants you to step out of the boat, like Peter did. Peter had to have looked foolish to the other disciples. But you know what? He is the only one who walked on the water. The key is to keep your eyes on Jesus, and trust Him to take care of you while you are learning and growing in these unfamiliar waters. Some people will think you are foolish, but that is their issue, not yours. When you stand before God, ultimately whose opinion is going to matter? Only God's right? Suddenly the opinions of your friends, family, or others that you were so worried about will no longer matter.

3. I Am Not Qualified

This is the biggest lie of all! If we believe that great exploits are only for the few, the chosen, and the specialists, then the everyday believer will DO nothing. God has called every day believers to participate, not to spectate. You are qualified. Jesus said so. He said, "these signs will accompany those who believe..." — **Mark**

16:17. You need to get this deep down in your heart. You are qualified because you are a believer. It does not

matter how old you are, how long you have been serving the Lord, or how great your speaking abilities are, etc. What qualifies you to lay hands on the sick is that you are believer in Jesus Christ. He paid the price for you with His blood. His blood covers you. That is what qualifies you. Art Thomas, a modern day healer tells stories of brand new believers being asked to pray for the sick, and they get immediate results. Why? They are believers, therefore, that qualifies them to pray for the sick. It does not matter if you have been in the kingdom five minutes or fifty years.

Now, this is really good news because it means that anybody can do it. God wants to use you to bring signs and wonders to your family, your friends, your work place, and your city. You! Yes, you! God wants to use you! Quit saying, "God won't use me." Remember that the power of life and death is in the tongue- **Proverbs 18:21**. If you speak it or say you cannot do it, then you believe you cannot do it. If you believe you cannot do it then you will not pray for anyone, therefore you have fulfilled your own prophetic statement about yourself when you said, "God cannot use me." God has not disqualified you. You have disqualified yourself.

Here are some ways that you can overcome these excuses.

1. Just do it- Grow in the Impossible

Remember the story from Chapter One about the father who brought his son to Jesus to be healed because he was having seizures caused by a demonic spirit? Jesus later told his disciples, after they asked how come they could not drive it out, that besides prayer and fasting, the problem was their lack of faith. When you go back and read the story from Matthew, Jesus' very first reaction to the father's statement, "I asked your disciples to drive it out, but they could not was, "Oh, you unbelieving and perverse generation, how long shall I stay with you? How long shall I put up with you?" - **Matthew 17:17** Who was he calling an unbelieving and perverse generation? This response was about His disciples. Why did Jesus respond so harshly? Here is why. He had been modeling for them. He showed them how to walk in the supernatural. Calling the Twelve to him, he began to send them out two by two and gave them authority over impure spirits- **Mark 6:7**. He trained them to do the same. He sent them out two by two, and they saw amazing results. The seventy-two returned with joy and said, "Lord, even the demons submit to us in your name" - **Luke 10:17** Jesus responded this way because all of their own experiences dealing with the supernatural along with them seeing all of the amazing things that Jesus did were supposed to build their faith. But He told them that they had very little faith **Matthew 17:20**-. He replied, "Because you have so little faith. Truly I tell you, if you have faith as small as a mustard seed, you can say to this mountain, 'Move from here to there,' and it will move. Nothing will be impossible for you."

For some reason, even after all they had personally experienced and witnessed, a lack of faith was still an issue. He told them that if they had faith as small as a mustard seed that nothing would be impossible for them. That gets me excited. I do not know about you, but I serve a God who can do the impossible, and I have signed on to participate in those impossibilities with Him. He has also recruited you to participate and no longer be a spectator. I love this story about John G. Lake, a healer from the turn of the century. This is an example of how we DO the Word and LIVE the Word, not just read the Word. John G. Lake, "tirelessly investigated the Bible with an eye not only to understand it, but to prove its accuracy in everyday life. As a result, Lake walked, talked, and breathed in the flow of God's resurrection life." Roberts Liardon — *God's Generals*. This inspires me! He not only wanted to understand God's Word, but he wanted to prove its accuracy. He did not just want to read about the miraculous, he wanted to live it and experience the same results that Jesus experienced.

Jesus promised to always be with us. His last words of the Great Commission are a promise that He will always be with us-**Matthew 28:20**. I find that comforting. He would not command us to do something and then send us out without His authority and presence. He has asked us to do the impossible. He knew we would need His presence to accomplish the impossible.

There is a story in the Old Testament in **Exodus 33** where God is deciding whether or not He will send His presence with the Israelite people because of their grumbling and complaining. God calls them a stiff-necked people. Moses prays to God and says, "If Your presence does not go with us, do not send us up from here." Moses knew that without the presence of God, there was no purpose in going. It would be futile. God heard the prayer of Moses and promised to go with them. Jesus does the same. He would not ask us to do anything without sending His presence with us. He equips us in every way to grow in the impossible.

Jesus wants our faith to grow. He sent his disciples out before they were ready. He created an environment where it was ok for them to make mistakes. He did not require perfection from them, but He did want them to grow, and He wanted their faith to grow. Jesus has done the same for you. That same environment that He created for His disciples to practice in is available to you. You have room to grow in the impossible. You have room to make mistakes. You have room to practice saying, "mountain move from here to there!" That excites me! God does not demand perfection from any of us. He just wants us to obey Him, to trust Him, and to grow. Just Do it! Live out God's Word like John G. Lake did. He read it, he believed it, and he practiced it. You have to start somewhere.

2. Understand That as Believers We Have a Responsibility

As believers in Jesus Christ, we have a responsibility to take action when we come into contact with the powers of darkness. We have a responsibility to release the Light into the darkness. Sickness and disease is darkness. We have a responsibility to pray for the sick. We are Jesus' plan A. There is no plan B. The Body of Christ is His plan to bring heaven to earth until He returns. God could choose to do everything Himself, but He didn't do it that way. He had a grand plan even before the foundations of the world, and His grand plan is YOU! He believes in you. He trusts you! There is a lost and dying world out there and we have the answer. Jesus commanded us to heal. Jesus lives in us so that as we go about our lives and run into darkness, He in us, transforms those situations. "He that is in me is greater than he that is in the world"- **1 John 4:4**. We have a responsibility to obey the command to go into all the world to fulfill the Great Commission, but we must not neglect the command to heal the sick. Healing is the answer to sickness just like forgiveness is the answer to sin. We have to quit making excuses that we are not ready. The disciples did not know all there was to know. They had room to grow and much more revelation to receive, but that did not stop Jesus from sending them out to train them. Always hold on to what Jesus said, "these signs shall follow those who believe." If you believe, if you pray, and if you take action, expect results. There is grace available to grow in this, and we have a responsibility as God's children to bring heaven to earth. We have the antidote to sickness and disease. His name is Jesus. We carry Him everywhere we go. Why would we withhold the solution? We need to put action to our faith and obey Jesus so that we can bring light into the darkest places. When we do that we can trust God to bring the increase. The story of Elisha is a great example of this principle. In **2 Kings 2** is the story of Elijah and Elisha. Elisha asked for a double portion of Elijah's anointing. Elijah promised Elisha that if he (Elisha) saw him when the Lord took him then what he had asked for would be granted. Elisha did see Elijah go up in the chariot of fire, and Elisha saw Elijah's mantle fall from the sky. Elisha went and picked it up. This mantle was a sign that he was getting exactly what he asked for. Now that he had it, what was he going to do? He immediately used what was given to him. He was "clothed with power from on high." He came to the Jordan, and now was the perfect time to use what was given to him. He struck the water with it, and the water parted. He received, and he used what was given to him. He had a responsibility to use what was given to him. So do you and I. The disciples were filled with *dunamis* power on the day of Pentecost; they were clothed with power from on high. They had a responsibility to steward what was given to them. They did and immediate results are documented in the book of Acts.

3. 1 Can Trust that Jesus Said, 'These Signs Will Accompany Those Who Believe."

What is stopping you from operating in the supernatural? What excuse are you embracing over the truth of the Gospel? When Jesus went about doing good and destroying the works of the devil, the dead were raised, the sick were healed, the demon-possessed were delivered, food/drink was multiplied, storms were stopped, and entire cities were transformed. Jesus said, "these signs shall accompany those who believe." I cannot stress that enough. You are qualified. Why? Because you are a believer in Jesus Christ. Belief is backed up by action. Believing something intellectually means nothing. Show me that you believe it by what you do. James, the brother of Jesus said in the book of James, "I'll show you my faith by what I do." We need to do the same. Demonstrate your faith by what you do.

The great T.L. Osborn and his wife Daisy once said in front of a crowd of around one thousand Muslims, "If God does not heal this man, do not believe a word I say." And then God showed up and the man they prayed for was healed! Wow! That is taking Jesus at His word. "These signs will accompany those who believe." That is faith, and you know that as soon as that healing happened, he had the undivided attention of 1,000 Muslims. Jesus himself said, in **John 10**: 'Do not believe me unless I do the works of my Father." That is a demonstration of absolute trust in God and His Word. We see this same concept in the story of when Elijah was on Mt. Carmel in front of all of the prophets of Baal. He was bold! He never doubted for a second that God would show up. In **1 Kings 18** it says 31Then Elijah said to all the people, "Come here to me." They came to him, and he repaired the altar of the Lord, which had been torn down. *'Elijah took twelve stones, one for each of the tribes descended from Jacob, to whom the word of the Lord had come, saying, "Your name shall be Israel." "With the stones he built an altar in the name of the Lord, and he dug a trench around it large enough to hold two seahs of seed. He arranged the wood, cut the bull into pieces and laid it on the wood. Then he said to them, "Fill four large jars with water and pour it on the offering and on the wood, "Do it again," he said, and they did it again. "Do it a third time," he ordered, and they did it the third time. "The water ran down around the altar and even filled the trench. At the time of sacrifice, the prophet Elijah stepped forward and prayed: "Lord, the God of Abraham, Isaac and Israel, let it be known today that you are God in Israel and that I am your servant and have done all these things at your command. 7Answer me, LORD, answer me, so these people will know that you, Lord, are God, and that you are turning their hearts back again." Then the fire of the Lord fell and burned up the sacrifice, the wood, the stones and the soil, and also licked up the water in the trench. When all the people saw this, they fell prostrate and cried, "The Lord—he is God! The Lord—he is God!"

Elijah wanted everyone on that mountain to know who God was. The prophets of Baal slashed themselves, called on the name of their god until noon, and danced around the altar but nothing happened. Elijah did everything he could to make sure that when God showed up (and Elijah knew He would) that it would be supernatural. There would be no way that a fire could be lit with all of that water poured in the trenches unless it was God Himself. Elijah prayed! God showed up! People fell on their faces declaring that God is God! Elijah expected God to show up, and God did!

Another example of bold faith is something John G. Lake did in 1910. John G. Lake went to Africa where the plague was ravaging the nation at that time. Lake and one of his associates volunteered to help free of charge to help go into homes and take out dead bodies and to bury them. During this time, the plague which was extremely contagious, never touched Lake. A doctor asked Lake what his secret was and Lake simply replied, "as I keep my soul in contact with the Living God so that His Spirit is flowing into my soul and body, that no germ will ever attach itself to me, for the Spirit of God will kill it." Lake wanted to show the doctor something amazing, so he had him get some of the living deadly germs out of the lungs of a deceased plague victim and put it under a microscope. The doctor complied. He saw that the germs were very much alive and active. Then Lake did something absolutely crazy. He told the doctor to put some on his (Lake's hand) and look at it under a microscope. He did and the doctor saw with his own eyes that the germs died instantly. There were other witnesses and yes, they were all amazed! I am amazed! That is a man who understands that "greater is He that

is in me than he that is in the world." He EXPECTED that those germs would die in his hand. That is a high level of expectation. He was living that verse, "these signs shall follow those who believe." I do not know about you, but that challenges me. |I want that kind of faith! The enemy has won if he can make you ineffective in the Kingdom of God. If he can keep you from praying for the sick, and keep you from going after more of God, then he has you right where he wants you. Do not buy in to his lies. I do not want the enemy to have any ground in my life. I don't think you do either. There is a lost and dying world around us and they are bound up in sickness, addiction, and they are demon possessed, and there are many that are not doing anything about it. God does not allow sickness. The church does when we do nothing about it. These signs will accompany those who believe. That is a promise. I hope your expectation level is challenged. God wants to use you, but the more important question is do you want Him to use you? Those who do not believe do not have. Those who keep making excuses will not have either. When the disciples saw the loaves and the fish, all they could see was they did not have. Jesus sees what you do have. If you have faith and obedience Jesus will multiply it and you will see that anything is possible. It is time that we flush every excuse down the toilet because that is where they belong. It is time for the Church to rise up and be the Greater Things Generation.

Excuses = Failure

- If it is important to you, you will find a way. If not, you will find an excuse.

- Excuses are the nails used to build the house of failure.

- Excuses are just lies wrapped up in pretty paper.

- He that is good at making excuses is seldom good for anything else. — Ben Franklin

- You can have results or excuses, not both.

- Excuses — they are for people who don't want it bad enough.

- Excuses are useless. Results are priceless.

"All the encouragement I need to minister to the sick is the ministry of Jesus. He worked the works of the Father as the eternal God, not a God adopting a temporary phase, putting on a show. God has no temporary phases. He is against suffering-it describes Him. It is a window into His counsels. It is His will. - Reinhard Bonnke

CHAPTER 3: LAY DOWN YOUR DOCTRINE AND PRECONCEIVED IDEAS

"Any revelation from God's Word that does not lead us into and encounter with God only serves to make us more religious. The church cannot afford 'form without power,' for it creates Christians without purpose." — Bill Johnson from When Heaven Invades Earth: A Practical Guide to a Life of Miracles

A Hunger for More

In the past eight years I have learned more than in the previous fifteen years of my walk with the Lord. In my quest to know more of God, I attended a School of Supernatural Ministry in 2011-2012 about forty miles from my home. On average, about eight hours a week I spent in classes learning so much more about God than I had ever been exposed to before. I was starving for more and I got it! I gobbled up every word. I studied and learned, and after nine months I left a completely different woman. In the eight years since, I have had a measure of breakthrough in walking in the supernatural. I discovered during that time of attending the school of supernatural ministry that I had received good teaching from my church, denomination, etc, but that was it. It could no longer satisfy! I wanted more than just good teaching.

I longed for experiences. I longed for encounters. I began to put myself in places where great men and women of God were who were currently experiencing amazing results. I wanted to learn all I could, and I did. I also learned about impartation. I received impartations from some amazing contemporary generals of the faith. I wanted all that I could get and I went after it. I wanted what they had to get on me. I immediately noticed a change. I learned to hear the voice of the Lord. I received more prophetic words than I ever had before. I developed a desire for miracles and healings more than I ever had before. God began to speak to me in my dreams like never before. I began to lay hands on people and see them healed. I began to get words of knowledge, and to prophesy over people. I desired more and more of God, and my heart burned to teach others to go after more of Him, to encounter Him, to seek Him, and to pray for the sick, etc.

Theology Challenged

During my time of attending the school, however, my theology was challenged. I was offended more often than not from the teachings I heard, and it drove me to search the scriptures to see if what I was hearing could possibly be the truth. It reminded me of the Bereans in the book of Acts. "For the Bereans were of more noble character than the Thessalonicans because they searched the scriptures to see if what Paul said was true." I would think things like, "Jesus heals sometimes, but not everyone gets healed, therefore, He must want some to be sick." Hindsight is always 20/20. I am so glad that my theology was challenged the way it was because I had to learn to lay down my theology and my doctrine in exchange for Him! I had to learn to lay down what I thought I knew and my preconceived ideas in exchange for truth and growth in my relationship with my Heavenly Father.

Jesus offended many to speak truth. He did not offend for the sake of offending, but he did challenge people's hearts. Much of what He taught caused many who were following Him to turn and walk away from Him. Let's look at an example.

In **John 6** it says, "Jesus said to them, 'Very truly I tell you, unless you eat the flesh of the Son of Man and drink his blood, you have no life in you. Whoever eats my flesh and drinks my blood has eternal life, and I will raise them up at the last day. For my flesh is real food and my blood is real drink. Whoever eats my flesh and drinks my blood remains in me, and I in them. Just as the living Father sent me and I live because of the Father, so the one who feeds on me will live because of me. This is the bread that came down from heaven. Your ancestors ate manna and died, but whoever feeds on this bread will live forever.' He said this while teaching in the synagogue in Capernaum."

Many Disciples Desert Jesus

On hearing it, many of his disciples said, "This is a hard teaching. Who can accept it?" Aware that his disciples were grumbling about this, Jesus said to them, "Does this offend you? Then what if you see the Son of Man ascend to where he was before! The Spirit gives life; the flesh counts for nothing. The words I have spoken to you—they are full of the Spirit and life. "Yet there are some of you who do not believe." For Jesus had known from the beginning which of them did not believe and who would betray him. He went on to say, "This is why I told you that no one can come to me unless the Father has enabled them." From this time many of his disciples turned back and no longer followed him. "You do not want to leave too, do you?" Jesus asked the Twelve. "Simon Peter answered him, "Lord, to whom shall we

go? You have the words of eternal life. We have come to believe and to know that you are the Holy One of God."

Here in this passage, Jesus was teaching them a deep spiritual truth, but many were offended at His words. They could not wrap their minds around what Jesus was saying. In verse **66** it says that many turned back and no longer followed Him. Their offense led them away from Jesus. No one there could fully comprehend the meaning of what Jesus was saying because it dealt with His upcoming death on the cross, and the blood He would later shed, but Peter's response to Jesus' question, "You do not want to leave too, do you?" is a lesson for each of us. Peter's basic response was (my paraphrase), "Lord, where are we going to go? You have the words of eternal life. We know who you are. We don't understand everything you say, but we trust in who you are."

Wow! If we could all respond like Peter when we don't understand. Staying rooted in Christ even when we don't understand everything is key. We must learn to run to Jesus when we do not understand something. Sometimes our natural minds do not understand spiritual principles. God says, "My ways are above your ways and my thoughts are higher than your thoughts." Your natural mind may not understand, but your spirit knows there is truth there. Submitting our thoughts and our limited intellect to the Supremacy of Christ is a must. Our intellect is not above God. We need to willingly lay down anything we do not understand at the feet of Jesus. We need to be like Peter and say, "Lord, I don't get it. I don't understand this, but I trust you. I trust in who you are. You are good! You love me. Teach me your ways, and open the eyes of my heart to help me understand." If we do not approach offense this way, then it can grow in our hearts and has the potential to lead us away from Jesus. We cannot allow anything we do not understand to draw us away from God. That is a strategy of the enemy. He uses offense as bait to get people to question God's character which can lead people to walk away from Jesus.

Incorrect Theology

Religion has the tendency to water down the truth. Religion is form without power. It is by nature intellectual, and if we do not allow the Word of God to point us to Jesus then we can get prideful and legalistic. Jesus rebuked the Pharisees on numerous occasions for having the law, but they never saw that the very fulfillment of the law, Jesus, was standing right in front of them. In **John 5:39-40** Jesus says, "You study" the Scriptures diligently because you think that in them you have eternal life. These are the very Scriptures that testify about me, yet you refuse to come to me to have life." I do not ever want to be that person that has religion and goes through the motions, but my heart is never changed. Sometimes in our quest to be right, we sacrifice truth. What is more important? Being right or seeking God to see if some of our own well-meaning ideas might be wrong? Sometimes you just might need to submit them to God and give Him a chance to change your heart. Allow the Holy Spirit to speak truth to you. We cannot allow any past experiences or any well-meaning teaching, or our own pride to lead us away from Jesus.

When it comes to miracles, for so long the church as a whole has created its own theology about why God does not heal. Why? To make ourselves feel better about things we cannot understand or explain. Chris Gore, a modern day healer says it this way, "The moment we get offended with God because we haven't seen what we have believed Him for is the moment we begin to operate out of unbelief, and before long we adjust our theology to suit our experience instead of adjusting our experience to the truth of the Gospel."

We must recognize when we do that. The enemy baits us and wants us to be offended at God because something did not happen the way we had faith that it would. We need to recognize that lie, cast it down, and instead realize that God's Word is still true, and even though we did not get what we hoped for, we must continue to believe God and pursue Him. Do not adjust your theology to suit your experience. Always adjust your experience to the truth of the Gospel. The root of adjusting your theology to suit your experience is unbelief. Disappointment causes us to doubt the goodness of God.

Correct Theology

Acts 10:38 says — "how God anointed Jesus of Nazareth with the Holy Spirit and power, and how he went around doing good and healing all who were under the power of the devil, because God was with him."

This verse says that Jesus went around doing good, and then the verse explains what the good things were that Jesus did. Very plainly in the verse, the good that Jesus did was healing all who were under the power of the devil. What were these things specifically? Healing the sick, delivering the oppressed, raising the dead. He was not just a benevolent man working at the food pantry or cleaning up trash in his community (not that these are bad things-I'm making a point here). It is very clear what these good works were. This very same scripture then says that he was healing all who were under the power of the devil. Well, then that tells me that sickness comes from the devil.

1 John 3:8 says, "The one who does what is sinful is of the devil, because the devil has been sinning from the beginning. The reason the Son of God appeared was to destroy the devil's work." How did Jesus destroy the devil's works? By healing the sick, delivering the oppressed, and raising the dead. Jesus said, "The Spirit of the Lord is on me, because he has anointed me to proclaim good news to the poor. He has sent me to proclaim freedom for the prisoners and recovery of sight for the blind, to set the oppressed free," **Luke 4:18**.

Many want to believe that it is God who gives sickness. If Jesus went about doing good, and healing people, etc, and if those very sicknesses that Jesus delivered people from were from God, then why would God send Jesus to earth to destroy the very sicknesses that God Himself gave? It does not make sense does it? Jesus made it very clear that He only did what He saw His Father doing. Jesus said that a house divided against itself cannot stand. He was saying that He and God would never work against each other. Everything they did, they did in tandem.

In **Luke 11** it says, "Jesus was driving out a demon that was mute. When the demon left, the man who had been mute spoke, and the crowd was amazed. But some of them said, "By Beelzebub, the prince of demons, he is driving out demons." Others tested him by asking for a sign from heaven.

Jesus knew their thoughts and said to them: "Any kingdom divided against itself will be ruined, and a house divided against itself will fall. ' If Satan is divided against himself, how can his kingdom stand? I say this because you claim that I drive out demons by Beelzebub. Now if I drive out demons by Beelzebub, by whom do your followers drive them out? So then, they will be your judges. But if I drive out demons by the finger of God, then the kingdom of God has come upon you."

We see that here Jesus is accused of driving out demons by the power of the devil. He makes it very clear that a house divided against itself cannot stand. He is saying, "Why would Satan drive out Satan?" He would not do that because it does not make any sense. Then Jesus drives his point home in verse 20 by saying that if He (Jesus) drives demons out by the power of God, then

the Kingdom of God has come upon them. Basically He was saying, "I drive out demons by the power of God. You have seen me do it, therefore, you have witnessed the power of God today." (My paraphrase) This is good theology: God and Jesus working together to combat sickness, disease, evil spirts, and death.

Exact Representation

In **Hebrews 1:3a** it says, "The Son is the radiance of God's glory and the exact representation of his being, sustaining all things by his powerful word."

If we want to know what God is like then all we have to do is look at the life of Jesus. Jesus is the exact representation of His being. Have you ever wanted to know what would God do in certain situations? Look at the life of Jesus and you have your answer. Does God like sickness? No! How do I know that? Jesus went about healing people. Does God like it when people are demon possessed? No, how do I know that? Jesus delivered those who were oppressed by demons and set them free. Does God like death? No! How do I know that? Jesus raised people from the dead and Jesus himself rose from the dead conquering sin and death. That is why God sent Jesus to earth — to combat suffering.

See? None of this is rocket science. We make it so much harder than it has to be. We must lay down our warped theology that Jesus wants us to be sick and that He is the one who gives it, and we need to quit thinking that it is not His will to heal. All of these are lies. He demonstrated the exact opposite in His earthly ministry, God is not a God who would give sickness and disease and then send Jesus to the earth to heal people of the very sicknesses and diseases that He gave. That is preposterous! God can only give what He has, and guess what? He is NOT sick. When Jesus arose from the grave, he was alive (not dead), without sin, and without sickness. It is the devil that comes to steal, kill, and destroy-**John 10:10**. Not God. The enemy has perverted the truth of the Gospel and somehow weaseled his way into the church and caused many to believe that sickness is from God, and that those who pray for healing or seek it are somehow from the devil. Jesus DID NOT come to destroy man, but to destroy the works of the devil. Jesus always brought the solution and the answer to help man. Healing is the answer to sickness and disease just like forgiveness is the answer to sin. Will you do the impossible and do these "greater things" that Jesus said we would do in John:14-12? Will you trust God enough to lay down what you do not understand and be willing to submit what you do not understand to Him? Will you be like Peter, and say, "Lord, I do not have all the answers, but I trust You. I will not walk away from you. I will continue to seek you even though I do not understand?"

I will fight for the truth of the Gospel, and I will not apologize for my position on this. God is good. The devil is not. God is not the author of sickness and disease. The devil is. God does not allow sickness so he can make people better. Can God get the glory from a sickness? Yes, He can because He is God and He can take what the enemy meant for harm and turn it around for good, but I will scream from the mountain tops that God is NOT the author of sickness and disease. He is good. How do I know this? "...Jesus went about doing good, destroying the works of the devil" — Acts

10:38.

Do Not Neglect Healing

I am convinced that not only do we need to preach the salvation message of the Gospel, but we can no longer neglect the healing message either. He is Jehovah Rapha which literally means, God Your Health! God is whole and He is healthy. He can only give what He has. He wants us to be whole and healthy as well. I want to help people truly understand that God is not punishing them with sickness. If people think that sickness is from God, then they will not pray for their healing! That is a lie from the pit of Hell! Do you see how the devil wins when we think like that?

I refuse to hold up the standard of the enemy. I will not perpetuate this lie or make excuses for why God does not heal when the Bible clearly teaches that Jesus healed, and He commanded us to do the same. I will hold up God's standard, and that is the only thing I will shoot for. We cannot lower our standards to please our flesh or our intellect when we cannot understand why someone is sick, dying, or did not get healed. That is a life without hope. God is looking for a people who will believe what He says and who will expect the miraculous and ACT! How can anyone get healed unless someone prays for them? Let's refuse to live without hope, but instead bring HOPE to a lost and dying world.

Jesus Paid the Price for Healing: It is Finished

Ponder this question. Why would Jesus spend most of His ministry doing things like healing the sick, delivering the oppressed, and raising the dead if it was all for nothing? It just does not make sense. We serve a God who knows how slow we can be sometimes. He is gracious and merciful. He leads the way. He demonstrated. He modeled. He knew we needed that. He did it all to show us that we should pursue the same things-**John 14:12**. Remember that everything flows from intimacy. In His overwhelming love for humanity, he paid the ultimate price for our salvation. The Greek word for salvation is Sozo. Sozo is an all-encompassing Greek word which means forgiven, healed, and delivered. Jesus' death on the cross paid for it all. The word sozo has been interpreted to only mean eternal life, but Jesus not only paid for our eternal life, He also paid the price for our healing.

In **Isaiah 53** it says, "Surely he took up our pain and bore our suffering, yet we considered him punished by God, stricken by him, and afflicted. But he was pierced for our transgressions, he was crushed for our iniquities; the punishment that brought us peace was on him, and by his wounds we are healed..."

1 Peter 2:24 -He himself bore our sins in his body on the cross, so that we might die to sins and live for righteousness; "by his wounds you have been healed."

Jesus was arrested, interrogated, and brutally beaten, and then He was forced to literally carry his cross for as long as He could until He could no longer endure the weight of it after the severe beating He had already taken. He was then nailed to that cross and suffered unimaginable pain. As He was dying on the cross He said, "IT IS FINISHED!" Why did He say that? Jesus was declaring from the cross that payment had been fully made for our SOZO, our forgiveness, healing, and deliverance! The very blood that Jesus shed on the cross not only paid for our forgiveness so that we may inherit everlasting life, but it was also payment rendered for our physical healing! It is time to give Jesus what He paid for.

Transfer of Authority

When Adam and Eve gave up their authority in the Garden of Eden, where did that authority go? Satan received that authority. **2Corinthians 4:4** says, "The god of this age has blinded the minds of unbelievers, so that they cannot see the light of the gospel that displays the glory of Christ, who is the image of God." Satan is the god of this age. Satan also told Jesus during His temptation in the desert that he would give Jesus all the Kingdoms of the world if Jesus would bow down and worship him because they (the kingdoms) had been given to him (Luke 4:6). Have you ever thought about that? How did he get them? By default - Adam and Eve forfeited their authority and that is how Satan received his authority.

Even though Satan does have a sphere of authority, we must understand that his authority is limited. Where does Satan reign? He reigns where he is allowed to reign. If believers in Jesus Christ do not walk in our God-given authority, then something else is allowed to rule. It is Satan's kingdom that is allowed to rule if we do not take dominion. That is how God's Kingdom works on earth. His Kingdom lives in every believer, and we have dominion, but we must enforce our authority. God's rule always trumps Satan's rule. We must kick Satan out where he has set up dominion.

In Matthew 16:18-19 it says, "I will give you the keys of the kingdom of heaven; whatever you bind on earth will be bound in heaven, and whatever you loose on earth will be loosed in heaven." And in Matthew 28:18 it says, "Then Jesus came to them and said, 'All authority in heaven and on earth has been given to me.'"

Jesus purchased that authority by His obedience to death on the cross! He made sufficient payment and gave us the keys! As believers in Jesus Christ we must understand that healing has been purchased and paid for. Cancer has been nailed to the cross. Diabetes has been nailed to the cross. Schizophrenia has been nailed to the cross! You name it! It has been nailed to the cross! It has been paid for. When we lay hands on the sick and pray it helps to know that what you are praying for has been purchased and paid for, and that it is under the blood, and that you have all authority to pray because Jesus died to give you that authority! When you pray for the sick you are declaring that the enemy must give Jesus what He already paid for. We can no longer exalt our well-intentioned but bad theology over the truth of the Word. We cannot exalt our preconceived ideas of healing or what we thought we knew over the truth of the Gospel. We need to get back to the basics and quit allowing the well-meaning but very wrong voices to tell us that Jesus no longer heals or that healing is from the devil. We need to lay down our theology and doctrine or any thoughts, teachings, etc. that are contrary to the Word of God.

CHAPTER 4- UNDERSTAND THAT JESUS IS WILLING

"The problem is not that His miracles have ceased but that we have failed to recognize His workings in the world...God's powerful hand of blessing is at work all around you, pouring out miracle after miracle." — Joan Hunter from Miracle Maintenance: How to Receive and Keep God's Blessings

Jesus Has Never Stopped Doing Miracles

God is good! All the time! Have you ever heard that expression? Jesus has never ceased doing miracles. The problem is that we, as His church, have failed to recognize them. God has never stopped being good. I heard something recently that I want to share with you that struck a chord deep in my spirit. I heard a man of God say that God showed him that many of His people are accusing Him (God) of Munchausen Syndrome by proxy. Munchausen Syndrome by Proxy is a mental disorder where a parent makes up or causes an illness in their own child by poisoning them or doing something else to cause them to be sick. It is a form of abuse.

Wow! Now that is a revelation. What parent would ever do that to their child? One that is mentally disturbed, right? How could God ever do that to His children? He wouldn't. Why? God is good. God is love. He would never keep us sick for His own pleasure. It goes against His very nature, and for us to believe that God would make us sick so then He can heal us later of something He caused is absolutely insane.

What do miracles reveal about God? What do they illustrate about His character? What is the purpose? The answers to these questions are that they demonstrate His absolute goodness! They demonstrate God's redemptive nature. They demonstrate His mercy and grace. They demonstrate His compassion. They demonstrate His desire to completely restore. They demonstrate that God is against suffering. And ultimately, miracles, signs, and wonders bring people to a place of decision. Jesus would often do supernatural works, and then He would teach the crowds because then He had their undivided attention. He would give them a demonstration of the Kingdom, and then give an explanation of the Kingdom. It was the demonstration of the Kingdom that brought people to a place where they had to choose.

Jesus said in John 10:37-38, "If I do not do the works of my Father, do not believe me, but If I do, though you do not believe me, believe the works that you may know and believe that the Father is in me, and I in Him."

To loosely paraphrase Jesus was saying, "Hey, these works that I'm doing prove that I come from God, but if you don't believe what I say, at least believe the works because they are absolute proof that I am in God, and that He is in me."

T.L. Osborn and his wife Daisy, during 1945 made a trip to India to preach the Gospel to Muslims. They stayed a little less than a year and unfortunately, they saw zero results. They came back to America very discouraged. They had such a heart to reach the Muslim people, so they prayed and sought God for an entire year asking God to show them what they needed to do differently to reach the people there. God showed T.L. that the answer was signs and wonders and miracles. God revealed that signs and wonders would be the key that would unlock the hearts of the Muslims they would minister to (Sid Roth's It's Supernatural June 15, 2015). God is willing to reach everyone. He wants all to come to the saving knowledge of His Son. He is willing to meet people right where they are, and doing the miraculous to unlock the hearts of those in darkness demonstrates His willingness. Isn't that awesome? That's the God that I serve. He is good!

Jesus Wants To Reveal His Glory

Jesus loves to manifest His glory. He is the Son of God. Miracles testify that He is who He says He is. He wants us to really KNOW who He is. He wants us to believe that He wants to heal! He wants us to know that He is willing to heal! He knows that when we really understand His willingness to heal that it will change the way see sickness and that will change the way we pray! Jesus' heart breaks for hurting people. Your helpless state before you became a Christian is what drove Him to the cross. People who are lost and dying will spend an eternity in hell. He paid the price so no one would have to spend an eternity separated from Him. That breaks his heart. Sickness, disease, and oppression also break His heart. He paid the price for that as well. He loves to heal. He wants to heal.

We are going to look at 9 New Testament examples to illustrate Jesus' willingness to heal.

Man with Leprosy Healed

1. Mark 1:40-44 says, "A man with leprosy came to him and begged him on his knees, 'If you are willing, you can make me clean.' 41 Jesus was indignant. He reached out his hand and touched the man. "I am willing," he said. 'Be clean!' Immediately the leprosy left him and he was cleansed."

I wanted to start with this one because it reveals Jesus' willingness. The man came to Jesus begging. He was desperate to be healed. "If you are willing," he said, "you can make me clean." He KNEW that Jesus had the power to do it. But he was not sure of Jesus' willingness to do it. Does this sound like anyone you know? There are so many that know that Jesus can, but there is a breakdown with the next part. They wonder if He is willing. Is this you? Has this ever been you? Have you ever thought like that? Jesus was indignant. He was frustrated that His willingness to heal was questioned. He wants people to understand that YES, He is willing. Sometimes we just need it spelled out for us. So, He says very plainly, "I am willing!" Jesus demonstrated compassion and He healed the man. Jesus is willing! No matter what! He does NOT delight in the suffering of mankind. He came to destroy the works of the devil, remember? Not to destroy man. It is a lie from the pit of hell to think otherwise.

Royal Official's Son is Healed

2. John 4:46-53 says, "Once more he visited Cana in Galilee, where he had turned the water into wine. And there was a certain royal official whose son lay sick at Capernaum. *' When this man heard

that Jesus had arrived in Galilee from Judea, he went to him and begged him to come and heal his son, who was close to death. '8 Unless you people see signs and wonders,' Jesus told him, 'you will never believe.' The royal official said, 'Sir, come down before my child dies.' 'Go,' Jesus replied, 'your son will live.' The man took Jesus at his word and departed. While he was still on the way, his servants met him with the news that his boy was living. When he inquired as to the time when his son got better, they said to him, 'Yesterday, at one in the afternoon, the fever left him.' Then the father realized that this was the exact time at which Jesus had said to him, 'Your son will live.' So he and his whole household believed."

Here is the story of a royal official desperate for Jesus to heal his son. I know often it can seem like Jesus is harsh, but He is targeting hearts with statements like "Unless you people see signs and wonders you will not believe." Jesus wanted to know if the man really believed that he could heal his son, or if he would be offended and walk away. The man did not even respond to Jesus' statement. He kept asking, "Come down before my child dies." That is what Jesus is looking for. Persistence! The man contended and went after his son's healing and He got it! Jesus demonstrated His willingness by healing the boy. There will always be opportunities for us to be offended at something. Whatever we focus on is what we will get. If we focus on our hurt, pain, and offense then that is what we will get, but if we are desperate and we allow that desperation to push us towards Jesus, we will get Jesus!

Jesus Heals Simon's Mother-in-Law

3. Luke 4:38-39 ~ "Jesus left the synagogue and went to the home of Simon. Now Simon's mother-in-law was suffering from a high fever, and they asked Jesus to help her. So he bent over her and

rebuked the fever, and it left her. She got up at once and began to wait on them."

Here in this very short passage, it was brought to Jesus' attention that Simon's mother-in-law was sick with a fever. They asked Jesus to help. So, what did he do? He helped her. He rebuked the fever and it left her. This clearly reveals that Jesus is loving, compassionate, and is willing to help people.

Jesus Heals Lame Man at Pool of Bethesda

4. In John 5:2-16 it says, "Now there is in Jerusalem near the Sheep Gate a pool, which in Aramaic is called Bethesda which is surrounded by five covered colonnades. Here a great number of disabled people used to lie—the blind, the lame, the paralyzed. When Jesus saw him lying there and learned he had been an invalid for thirty-eight years he waked him, "Do you want to get well?" "Sir, he replied, "I have no one to help me into the pool when the water is stirred. While I am trying to get in, someone else goes down." Then Jesus said to him, "Get up! Pick up your mat and walk."

At once the man was cured; he picked up his mat and walked. He wanted to get well because he was there where the supernatural waters were stirring, but in his condition he could never make it into the water first. I love that in this account, Jesus saw him. Jesus notices people. He cares about people. Jesus noticed this man and then Jesus asked some questions and discovered that this man had been in this condition for a very long time. Jesus approached him and asked him if he wanted to get well. The man did NOT answer the question. It was a yes or no question. He gave Jesus an excuse as to why he could not get in the water. He was looking for sympathy. Jesus spoke to him and said,"Get up! Pick up your mat and walk." And the man was cured!

Jesus had compassion on this man! He noticed him out of all of those other people. He then approached him, spoke with him, and healed him! Jesus initiated that entire healing. Jesus demonstrated His willingness to heal! Jesus offers something better than sympathy. He offers complete healing!

Jesus Heals Man with Shriveled Hand In the Synagogue

5. Matthew 12:9-13 "Going on from that place, he went into their synagogue, and a man with a shriveled hand was there. Looking for a reason to bring charges against Jesus, they asked him, "Is it lawful to heal on the Sabbath?" He said to them, "If any of you has a sheep and it falls into a pit on the Sabbath, will you not take hold of it and lift it out?" How much more valuable is a person than a sheep! Therefore it is lawful to do good on the Sabbath." Then he said to the man, "Stretch out your hand." So he stretched it out and it was completely restored, just as sound as the other."

In this particular passage you have Jesus healing a man's hand on the Sabbath. Jesus cared very much about this man. This healing demonstrates Jesus' love for the individual. The teachers of the law demanded that one should honor the Sabbath above people. Jesus blew their theology right out of the water! "How much more valuable is a person than a sheep?" What is most important is an individual with a need. Jesus met this man's need and healed him. Jesus demonstrated his willingness to heal no matter who it offended.

Jesus Heals Two Blind Men

6. In Matthew 9:27-31 it says, "As Jesus went on from there, two blind men followed him, calling out, "Have mercy on us, Son of David!" 8 When he had gone indoors, the blind men came to him, and he asked them, "Do you believe that I am able to do this?" "Yes, Lord," they replied. Then he touched their eyes and said, "According to your faith let it be done to you"; and their sight was restored.

Here, Jesus responds to the two men asking Him for mercy. The question Jesus asks them is, "Do you believe that I am able to do this?" They respond with a resounding YES! He touches their eyes and told them that according to their faith they were both healed. Jesus demonstrated His willingness to heal by stopping his life, and taking time to show mercy on these two men who were desperate to see. He proved again that He is willing.

Jesus Raises a Young Boy from the Dead at his Own Funeral

7. In Luke 7:11-17 it says, "Soon afterward, Jesus went to a town called Nain, and his disciples and a large crowd went along with him. As he approached the town gate, a dead person was being carried out—the only son of his mother, and she was a widow. And a large crowd from the town was with her. When the Lord saw her, his heart went out to her and he said, "Don't cry." Then he

went up and touched the bier they were carrying him on, and the bearers stood still. He said, "Young man, I say to you, get up!" The dead man sat up and began to talk, and Jesus gave him back to his mother. They were all filled with awe and praised God. "A great prophet has appeared among us," they said. "God has come to help his people." This news about Jesus spread throughout Judea and the surrounding country."

In this example, Jesus is traveling through this town where he sees a funeral procession. Jesus was watching the scene unfold before Him, but when he saw the mother of the dead boy, his heart went out to her. He was filled with compassion for her. He told her not to cry and then he touched the boy, and told him to get up. The boy was resurrected immediately, and Jesus gave him back to his mother. Besides Jesus raising him from the dead, I am moved by the words, "and Jesus gave Him back to his mother." Jesus is the great Restorer! He loves to restore life, and relationships. Wow! Jesus was so moved by the grief of the mother that He stopped His life and intervened in this situation. No one asked him to. Jesus is willing!

Jesus Delivers Woman from a Crippling Spirit

8. Luke 13:10-13 "On a Sabbath Jesus was teaching in one of the synagogues, and a woman was there who had been crippled by a spirit for eighteen years. She was bent over and could not straighten up at all. When Jesus saw her, he called her forward and said to her, "Woman, you are set free from your infirmity." Then he put his hands on her, and immediately she straightened up and praised God.

In this example Jesus again heals on the Sabbath. He sees a woman who had been crippled by a demonic spirit for eighteen years. Jesus calls her forward and sets her free. This is another healing where no one is asking Jesus to heal. Jesus notices this woman, sees that her problem is caused by a spirit, so, he initiates the healing and sets the woman free. Jesus is willing.

Jesus Delivers Boy from a Demonic Spirit

9. In Mark 9 a father brings his child to Jesus to be healed of demonic spirit. In verse 21, "Jesus asks the boy's father, "How long has he been like this.' 'From childhood,' he answered. 'It has often thrown him into the fire or water to kill him. But if you can do anything, take pity on us and help us.' 'If you can?' said Jesus. 'Everything is possible for him who believes.' Immediately the boy's father exclaimed, "I do believe; help me overcome my unbelief!"

In these verses Jesus repeats the man's question, "If you can?" out loud. The statement "if you can" is very telling about what was in the man's heart. He just was not quite sure if Jesus could, but he sure wanted Jesus to try. Jesus then responds, "Everything is possible for him who believes." The man's response was amazing. He wanted Jesus to help him overcome his unbelief. Jesus then rebuked the Spirit, and it left the boy. Jesus is willing to heal. He really does WANT to.

I could go on and on using examples from the scriptures to explain Jesus' willingness to heal, but as you examine the scriptures for yourself you will discover that He is! Do not ever let anyone tell you that He is not. He loves people. He is willing! Those are His own words. He said, "I am willing." What other evidence do we need? He came to destroy the works of the devil, not to destroy people. He came to set the captives free. Let that resonate deep down in your soul.

Keep Knocking on the Door of Healing

I read this quote by Randy Clark and it deeply affected me. He says in *Healing Unplugged: Conversations and Insights from Two Veteran Healing Leaders* "...that same month, January 1995, and I saw more miracles in that time than I had seen in the first 24 years put together!...The only thing I can attribute it to was that for 24 years I had been knocking on the door of healing, and God came."

I absolutely love this statement. We need to keep knocking on the door to healing. As believers in Jesus Christ we need to know that He is willing. We need to keep knocking. What keeps us knocking is His willingness. He will show up! Breakthrough is waiting for those who will keep knocking. "Ask, and it will be given to you, seek, and you will find, knock and the door will be opened to you." Matthew 7:7

When I believed that Jesus was not willing and I wondered whether or not it was His will or not to heal, I never saw results, however, now that I believe that He is willing, and I expect Him to heal, now when I pray I see God move like never before and people get healed. I pray more than ever and I see more results than I ever have before.

I prayed for a lady that I attended church with one time. She had been to the doctor because she was in a lot of pain with kidney stones. X-rays showed several stones. I laid hands on her and I prayed. I commanded the stones would dissolve in Jesus' name! She went back to the doctor because she was scheduled for surgery, and when the doctors went in to remove the stones, they could not find them. We serve an amazing God! Let's quit accusing God of Munchausen's Syndrome by proxy. He does not find pleasure in hurting His children. He is a good God and He is willing to heal. He wants us to BELIEVE that He can heal, and that He WANTS to heal. HE IS WILLING!

When you begin to pray for others, knowing that Jesus is willing will give you more confidence to take dominion over the darkness you are praying against. Knowledge is power. Now you are armed with the knowledge that Jesus is willing.

CHAPTER 5: UNDERSTAND YOU HAVE AUTHORITY TO COMMAND AND MAKE DECLARATIONS

"You can take back what has been stolen when you realize you were created for recovery."-Cal Pierce

As Christians, we are the light of the world. We were created for purpose. Just as Cal Pierce says in the opening quote, as believers in Jesus Christ, we were created for recovery. Jesus started the recovery process by his death and resurrection and He passed that same ministry on to you and me. Jesus conquered the grave! He purchased ALL authority and has given it to us, His Bride. We get to play a part in recovering ALL that the enemy has stolen from us and we get to help others in their recovery process as well. We get to take back things that the enemy has stolen. We have permission to march directly into the enemy's camp and take back what is rightfully ours.

Going Beyond the Enemy's Front- Line Defense

The term breakthrough is a military term and is defined as "to advance through and beyond the enemy's front line of defense; to overcome every obstacle, barrier, and hindrance to progress." D-Day, the day of military attack of American and British Allied Forces that invaded German occupied France on June 6, 1944 was the beginning of the end of World War II. If the Allied Forces would have stopped fighting on that day, thinking they had complete victory, they would not have won the war. That day on the beaches of Normandy, though it was a monumental day, was just the beginning of the end. The war would not end until over a year later in September of 1945. As believers, fighting against the dark powers of Satan, we must take the "beaches at Normandy" so to speak, in the Spirit, and we must battle beyond the beaches to the end of the war. We must push through the initial breakthrough and go BEYOND the enemy's front line of defense.

Called Out Ones

You and I are ambassadors for His Kingdom. We have the highest honor which is to represent God in this sinful world. As ambassadors of His Kingdom, we have been given the
authority to represent the Kingdom of God. He has given us everything we need to represent Him accurately. Just like Jesus is the exact representation of the Father, we are also to represent Jesus accurately, and do the things He did. Jesus did only what He saw the Father do, and said only what He heard the Father say. The word "ecclesia," the Greek word we use for "church," means "called out ones."

It was a cultural term of the day in Greece meaning "civil assembly of called out people who were given political power and juridical functions." They were a body of legislators. They had authority to allow things or to forbid things. The Romans also used the term "ecclesia," and it was a military term. It also means "called out ones", but in this case it referred to those who were called out of the general armed forces population and assigned to a special task force. These were those in the Roman Army who had a special assignment. They would be assigned to a certain territory or land, and they were to take the land and rule their assigned territory. Their job was to replicate Rome. They were to replicate Rome in their assigned territories. Both of these definitions capture the essence of our assignment here on earth as followers of Jesus Christ. We are "the called out ones." We have been given authority from heaven to allow or to forbid (to bind and loose).

Every time we "declare," we are coming into agreement with what God says on a matter. We are allowing His Kingdom to rule on the earth, and forbidding the enemy to have rule. It's a legal contract we are entering into when we bind and loose. The same is true of the second definition of "ecclesia." Jesus has given us all authority to replicate His Kingdom on earth. Wherever we are physically on the earth our job is to "replicate His Kingdom," just like the special task force of "eccelsia" were to take the land and to replicate Rome. When we come into contact with darkness we have authority and dominion over that darkness because the same Holy Spirit that raised Jesus from the dead is the same Holy Spirit that lives in you and me.

The Lord's Prayer

-HOW we Pray, not WHAT we Pray

When we understand what we were created for, it changes the way we see a problem, and it changes the way we approach the problem. Jesus taught us how to pray. Let's look at the model prayer that Jesus taught his disciples to pray. I want to point out that this is a prayer that Jesus taught them HOW to pray, not word for word WHAT to pray. Jesus was never interested in us repeating a thoughtless prayer over and over again. He could not have wanted that from his disciples when he rebuked the religious leaders of his day for doing exactly that. Jesus is not interested in any ostentatious prayers. Instead, He is interested in our hearts and He is interested that we are connecting with Him. We have the liberty and freedom to make declarations when we pray. We do not have to ask God's permission to heal. We have the freedom to declare and command. Making declarations is powerful. Let's look at the Word to help teach this point In Matthew 6:9-13 Jesus teaches his disciples what is commonly known as The Lord's prayer.

We are going to break down this prayer and talk about each part.

1. "Our Father, who is in heaven, hallowed be your name."

Obviously this verse means exactly what it says. When we pray we should always go to God as our Father. Not some distant cold Father, but as our Daddy God! Our Abba God. In the Old Testament, there is no reference of addressing God in such a childlike informal way, but Jesus introduces us to God in a brand new way. God has reintroduced Himself to His children. Jesus introduces us to our Daddy God. The Bible is a progression of the revelation of God. Jesus unveils to us that God, our Heavenly Father, is our Daddy. He's warm and inviting and He extends an invitation to us to run to Him like a child and jump into His lap and tell Him about our day while He listens intently to every word. He is a loving Daddy who loves to hold us, listen to us, and talk with us. Even though He is our Daddy, we should approach Him understanding who He is which is holy and pure. But even though He is holy and His name is holy, He is approachable. The book of Hebrews tells us to "boldly approach the throne of grace." When we come to our Holy Daddy God, we need to understand that He is a God that has an abundance of grace for His children, and He absolutely loves it when we boldly come to Him!

2."Your Kingdom come, Your will be done, on EARTH AS IT IS IN HEAVEN."

This is a declaration in itself. We have permission to pray basically, "Daddy God, allow your will to be done in this situation and I know your will is to release heaven to earth." What does heaven have? Love, joy, peace, health, wholeness, LIFE... that is what heaven has. When we pray and make declarations for God's will to be done "on earth as it is in heaven" we are extending His royal rule to earth. This is so important for each of us to understand because when we really get this and really understand the extent of our authority then we will become bolder in the way we pray because we understand that when we pray we are extending His kingdom to earth. We have the great privilege to call down heaven and release it into whatever situation we may be facing.

3. "Give us our daily bread."

This is also a declaration. He is saying that we can talk to God about our daily provision. We have permission to say, "God, provide everything I need for this day." Do you know why we get to declare this so boldly? Because it is his desire to provide for His children, and He loves to meet our needs. One day at a time is all we need to be concerned about. We do not have to worry about tomorrow or the next day. Jesus even said that worrying does not add a single hour to our lives. We accomplish nothing by worrying about our needs. We get to boldly approach the throne of grace and talk to God about providing all that we need for each day.

4. "Forgive us our debts, as we have also forgiven our debtors."

Here is another declaration. Jesus taught us to pray to God to forgive us of our sins, just as we have forgiven those who have sinned against us. This is crucial for every believer to understand. We must learn to extend forgiveness in order to receive
forgiveness. Who are we to accept forgiveness from God, but then to turn around and **withhold forgiveness from those who have hurt us, rejected us, abused us, etc?**

Let's look at another story in the Bible from Matthew 18 that will help us understand God's heart on this matter. Then Peter came to Jesus and asked, "Lord, how many times shall I forgive my brother or sister who sins against me? Up to seven times?" Jesus answered, "I tell you, not seven times, but seventy-seven times." "Therefore, the kingdom of

heaven is like a king who wanted to settle accounts with his servants. "As he began the settlement, a man who owed him ten thousand bags of gold" was brought to him. Since he was not able to pay, the master ordered that he and his wife and his children and all that he had be sold to repay the debt. "At this the servant fell on his knees before him. 'Be patient with me,' he begged, 'and I will pay back everything.' " The servant's master took pity on him, canceled the debt and let him go.
"But when that servant went out, he found one of his fellow servants who owed him a hundred silver coins." He grabbed him and began to choke him.'Pay back what you owe me!' he demanded. "His fellow servant fell to his knees and begged him, 'Be patient with me, and I will pay it back.' "But he refused. Instead, he went off and had the man thrown into prison until he could pay the debt. When the other servants saw what had happened, they were outraged and went and told their master everything that had happened. "Then the master called the servant in. 'You wicked servant,' he said, 'I canceled all that debt of yours because you begged me to. Shouldn't you have had mercy on your fellow servant just as I had on you?' "In anger his master handed him over to the jailers to be tortured, until he should pay back all he owed. "This is how my heavenly Father will treat each of you unless you forgive your brother or sister from your heart."

In this parable this man was forgiven of what would translate into a ten million dollar debt in today's currency. That's some forgiveness isn't it? He was not going to have to pay a dime of the massive debt he owed. He begged for mercy and was generously forgiven. He gladly received the mercy offered to him, however, even though he was so generously forgiven, he immediately goes to someone who owes him about what would be ten dollars in today's money. He demands payment from this individual. The man who owed him the money begged for mercy but he refused to give him mercy. Instead he has him imprisoned. The generous man who had forgiven him of his ten million dollar debt finds out about the man refusing mercy to the one who owed such a small amount. He calls him a wicked servant and has his imprisoned until he pay backs every dime. Jesus makes it very clear that when we receive God's forgiveness and then turn around and withhold forgiveness from others, we are being exactly like the unmerciful servant in this parable. So when Jesus teaches his disciples how to pray in the Lord's Prayer, the lesson is to be generous in extending forgiveness. Everything else flows from intimacy. Forgiveness flows from intimacy. The same Holy Spirit that raised Jesus from the dead lives in every believer. Forgiveness comes from Him, and should flow through us. It is supernatural. God is love. If we are "in Him," and "He is in us," then His character will also flow from us. He is generous when it comes to forgiveness, and so should we.

5. "Lead us not into temptation, but deliver us from evil."

Another declaration! It's a prayer that says, "God, lead me away from temptation, but if I am tempted, deliver me from it, and when the enemy is trying to hurt me, and get me to stumble, deliver me."

The Lord's prayer is a prayer that Jesus taught us to pray. Again, it is HOW he taught us to pray, not WHAT He taught us to pray, meaning we do not have to recite this prayer word for word until it means absolutely nothing. It is a model prayer. Jesus was illustrating that as we pray, we should focus on:

1. God's holiness, but also His accessibility. He is our Daddy God.

2. Bringing Heaven down to earth. Releasing Heaven into whatever situation we are in. Extending His rule/His Kingdom into this one! We are an extension of His hand.

3. Talking to God about the provision we need each day.

4. Forgiveness. Forgiveness from God, and forgiving others.

5. Deliverance. Divine protection from temptation and the evil one.

Declaring is coming into agreement with what God has already said. Some are under the impression that we have no business declaring and commanding. They think we have no right to tell God what to do. They believe that declaring and commanding is crossing a boundary. They see it as bossing God or telling God what to do. Nothing could be further from the truth. We are coming into alignment with God, and following Jesus' example when we make declarations. When we make declarations we are "boldly approaching the throne of grace." Jesus modeled it for us.

He knew who He was and because Jesus understood who He was and understood His mission He was not afraid to confront darkness when He saw it and when He did He called heaven to earth and darkness fled. When we really discover who we are and what God has called us to, we will understand that we have every right to make declarations. When we do not know who we are in Christ, our prayers our puny and powerless. But we discover who we really are in Christ, our prayers become much more powerful and effective. It's not God we are bossing. It is darkness that we are commanding to go.

Identity Crisis = Divided Prayers

Identity crisis causes us to pray with divided hearts. Divided prayers will accomplish nothing. That is NOT faith! We get what we expect. If our prayers are divided that means we are doubting God will show up, and if we doubt, then our prayers are powerless. God wants us to pray targeted prayers, and declarations are exactly that. We are aiming at the bullseye, and our declaration is the arrow leaving our bow. Declaring the works of the Father comes from this place of knowing exactly who our Daddy is, and knowing that as His child, we have access to everything He has because our Daddy is generous. The story of the Prodigal Son in Luke 15 is a great illustration of this point. "But the father said to his servants, 'Quick! Bring the best robe and put it on him. Put a ring on his finger and sandals on his feet. Bring the fattened calf and kill it. Let's have a feast and celebrate. For this son of mine was dead and is alive again; he was lost and is found.' So they began to celebrate. Meanwhile, the older son was in the field. When he came near the house, he heard music and dancing. So he called one of the servants and asked him what was going on. 'Your brother has come,' he replied, 'and your father has killed the fattened calf because he has him back safe and sound.' The older brother became angry and refused to go in. So his father went out and pleaded with him. But he answered his father, 'Look! All these years I've been slaving for you and never disobeyed your orders. Yet you never gave me even a young goat so I could celebrate with my friends. But when this son of yours who has squandered your property with prostitutes comes home, you kill the fattened calf for him!' My son,' the father said, 'you are always with me, and everything I have is yours. But we had to celebrate and be glad, because this brother of yours was dead and is alive again; he was lost and is found."

I want to look at the behavior of the oldest son here to illustrate my point. The Father was so ecstatic that His lost son was finally home that He threw a party to celebrate his homecoming! The older son was angry because he did not think such behavior warranted a celebration, and he complained that his father had never thrown him such a celebration.

The Father made a revelatory comment to his older son, "You are always with me, and everything I have is yours." Go back and read that again. He said, "Everything I have is yours." The older son always had access to everything His Father had, but all he could focus on was what he did not have and what his father never did for him. His dad was saying, (my paraphrase) "Son, everything that is mine is yours. If you wanted a goat to celebrate with your friends, then you should have just taken one because what is mine is yours. It always has been." We have access to everything that is the Father's. As God's children we have access to everything that Jesus had access to. Are you hearing that? He could just take what was rightfully his. When we declare and command that is exactly what we are doing... taking what is rightfully ours! But because the older son did not really understand this, he missed out on what was rightfully his the whole time, and it affected his attitude. Not knowing who our Daddy really is can make us angry and resentful, and extremely judgmental. I want you to get through your head that it is Biblical to Make Declarations. You are allowed.

Let's look at some examples from Jesus' ministry and some New Testament Church examples to demonstrate the power of this concept of making declarations. It is Biblical. Jesus himself told his disciples they could make declarations. He told them in Matthew 17, "If you say to this mountain be moved from here to there, then it will obey you." He did not say that, "if you ask God to move this mountain from here to there, maybe He will move it." No, He told them to SAY...to DECLARE!

Here are some declarations of Jesus. Remember that Jesus is our model. He was a man, full of the Holy Spirit accomplishing these things. In all of these examples, people were healed. The focus is the declaration that was made in each. You can look up the other details of each healing.

1. John 4:46-53. Jesus says, "Go, your child will live."

2. Luke 4: 33-36. In verse 33 Jesus told the demon to "Be quiet." And then He told it, "Come out of him."

3. Luke 4:38-39, Matthew 8:14-15; Mark 1:30-31 - Jesus REBUKED the fever and it left.

4. Matthew 8:16-17, Mark 1:32-34, Luke 4: 40-41-Jesus drove out the evil spirits with a word.

5. Matthew 8:2-4, Mark 1:40-44, Luke 5:12-15-Jesus said "Be clean!"

6. Matthew 9:2-8, Mark 2:3-12, Luke 5:18-26-Jesus heals a paralyzed man. Makes no distinction between forgiveness of sins and healing. He says, "your sins are forgiven,"and "Take up your mat and walk."

7. John 5:2-16-"...asked him a question, and then said, "Get up! Pick up your mat and walk."

8. Matthew 8:5-10; Luke 7: 2-10-"Go, it will be done just as you believed."

9. Luke 7:11-15-"I say to you, get up."

10. Mark 5:1-13-"Come out of this man, you impure spirit."

11. Mark 7:32-37-"Be opened."

12. Matthew 17:14-21, Mark 9: 17-29, Luke 9:38-43-"You deaf and mute spirit, I command you, come out of him and never enter him again."

13. John 11:1-44-"Take away the stone." "Lazarus come out." "Take off grave clothes."

14, Mark 10:46-52, Luke 18:35-43-To blind Bartamaeus, Jesus says, "Go. Your faith has healed you.

New Testament Church Examples

Jesus modeled it, and now you see here the early church following Jesus' example in making declarations.

15. Acts 3:1-7-Peter said, "In the name of Jesus Christ of Nazareth, WALK!"

16. Acts 4:29-41-the disciples prayed, "Stretch out your hand to heal and perform miraculous signs and wonders through the name of your holy servant Jesus." Then the **place was shaken and they were all filled with the Holy Spirit and spoke the Word** boldly.

17. Acts 5:12-(this was a result of the declaration they made in prayer in Acts 4) the apostles performed many miraculous signs and wonders among the people...and more and more men and women were added to their number.

18. Acts 9:32 -Aeneas, a paralytic was bed ridden eight years. Peter said, "Jesus Christ heals you. Get up and take care of your mat."

19. Acts 9:36-43-Peter raises a girl from the dead. He said, "Tabitha, get up," and she did.

20. Acts 14:8-a crippled man in his feet from birth was listening to Paul preach, and Paul **saw that he had faith to be healed and he said, "stand up on your feet,"** and he was healed.

We would never be asked to do something that wasn't first demonstrated to us by Jesus and the early church. What I am sharing with you is clearly Biblical. It is the model. Making declarations is part of our assignment! When we make declarations we are coming into alignment with our orders from The Commander of the Lord's Army. He told us to. It is a Biblical concept. It is imperative that we obey His orders.

Ezekiel's Vision

We see in the old Testament what God tells Ezekiel in a vision to further illustrate this point:

SAY To These Bones, LIVE!

In Ezekiel 37 the prophet Ezekiel has a vision. He sees a valley of dry bones. In Ez 37: 3-7 The Lord asks Ezekiel, "Can these bones live?" Ezekiel responds diplomatically to God's question. "O Sovereign Lord, you alone know." Then God tells Ezekiel, "Prophesy to these bones and SAY to them, 'Dry bones, hear the Word of the Lord! This is what the Sovereign Lord says to these bones: I will make breath enter you and you will come to life. Then you will know that I am the Lord.' So I prophesied as I was commanded." The rest of the story is that those bones came together and came to life and formed a vast army. Do you see that? He prophesied as He **was commanded!**

Declarations are prophetic! The power of our declarations causes dead things to come to life. Our declarations cause the sick to become healed, and our declarations cause demons to flee! It is time that we begin to bind and loose and make declarations to bring Light into the earth. Remember Jesus said in Luke 17, "If you SAY to this mulberry bush, be uprooted and be planted into the sea, it will obey you." When your child misbehaves do you ask the child, "Would you like to go to your room?" No, you declare, "Go to your room," and your child obeys because he/she knows you mean business. There is power in the declaration!

Make A New Decree

I want to end this chapter with some truths we can learn from the Book of Esther. The entire book of Esther is the story of a young woman who was put into a position as Queen, but who withholds her true identity from her husband, The King of Persia. She realizes that she must reveal who she really is so that she can save her people because a wicked man named Haman has made a decree in the King's name that on a certain day all Jews must be annihilated. Esther prays and fasts. With encouragement from her Uncle Mordecai, she knows that she must speak to the King, but there is a problem. She has not been invited into the King's presence for almost a month, and by law, if anyone goes to the King's presence without being summoned, or invited, they could lose their life. Esther takes a huge chance and even boldly declares, "If I perish, I perish," but she knew that she had to take the chance to save her people. She enters the King's throne room uninvited. Now, the King could extend his golden scepter to anyone who did that, and if he did so, that means that their life would be spared, but if he did not, the result was execution.

Esther boldly stood at the entrance of his throne room until he saw her. As a matter of fact in **Hebrew, upon seeing Esther, it says, "she lifted up favor in His eyes." He was not** offended that she was there. He looked favorably upon her. He extended the golden scepter to her. The king knew that Esther never would have taken that chance if it was not regarding some pressing issue, so he asked her what she wanted. He said she could ask anything she wanted and he would give it to her. She did not tell him right then what she wanted, but what she did was invite him and Haman to a banquet she was having that night. He agreed to come and to bring Haman. At the banquet that evening, he asked her again what she wanted, and he said that she could ask anything, and he would grant her request. Instead of revealing her request then, she invited he and Haman to another banquet that she would have the following the day. The next day, at the Banquet, Esther asks the King to spare her life and the life of her people, and that Haman has plotted and decreed that all of her people shall be annihilated on a certain day. The King became furious at this. He did not realize that Haman had made this decree, and he did not realize that his queen was Jewish. Haman realizes that the King has already decided his fate, and he falls on Esther begging for his life, and at that very moment, the King walks in and sees Haman on his wife. Haman is taken immediately by the King's officials and executed. In Persia at this time, once the King made a decree, he could not nullify or reverse it, so he tells Esther to make a new decree! Esther and Mordecai write a new decree declaring that all Jews had the right to defend themselves and to fight back, kill, and destroy anyone who tried to hurt them. The end of the story is that the Jews were victorious. An entire nation of people was saved because of a girl who did not value her own life over her people's lives. "For such a time as this," she was brought into the King's palace.

I want you to understand what God has revealed to His church through this story of Esther in the Old Testament. God is telling you that first of all, you have permission to approach Him, and when you do, you lift up favor in His eyes. He loves it when you come to Him. You can boldly approach Him. Secondly, He is telling you that He will give you what you ask for because it is within His power to give. Nothing is impossible for Him. And last of all, He is telling you to make a new decree! The enemy has decreed things over people. He has decreed that people will be sick. He has decreed that people shall suffer. He has decreed that people will be caught up in addiction, pornography, sexual sin, etc. But you have the privilege to make a new decree! A new command! A new declaration! And God wants you to know that He has signed off on your decree with His signet ring! His blood! Your decree has value because He has already and purchased what you are declaring. You get to be involved in the recovery process! As you decree, command, and declare people will get set free! You have permission from The King of Kings and Lord of Lords to make declarations! So, just as Esther was put into a position as Queen for such a time as this" to save her people from annihilation, it is for such a time as this, you have been raised up in His Kingdom!

CHAPTER 6: BE A CONTENDER

"There is something about believing God that will cause Him to pass over a million people to get to you." -Smith Wigglesworth

God Likes When We Contend

At a conference I attended, I heard a story from one of the speakers. He told a story of a seven year period when he was extremely sick. He had lost so much weight that he dropped to under 100 pounds, had no appetite, and he was so weak that his wife had to help him go to the restroom. During this awful time, like any good Christian would, he prayed. He says that he spent thousands of hours praying. During these prayer times he repented of anything and everything he could think of. He forgave anyone he might have unforgiveness toward, and he still was not healed. He tried to cover all of his bases so that he could receive his healing, but to no avail. Obviously, after so much time being sick, and after thousands of hours praying with absolutely no change, he was extremely frustrated and became really angry. One day he had had enough, and in his anger he confronted God. He said something really bold. He told God that He was not doing His job. He held God accountable to His Word. He knew God was His healer. The confrontation he had with God that day changed everything. That day was the beginning of his healing. Why am I telling you this story? God desires truth in the inmost parts —Psalm 51:6. He wants us to be real with Him. He already knows what is in our hearts. Even though we may not say it out loud, He knows. This man was fed up and angry that he was getting absolutely nowhere as he prayed. He knew that God was The Great Physician, but he was not getting healed. He knew that God could do the impossible, but the impossible was not happening in his life. This provoked his anger because He knew that God's Word said, "Praise the Lord, my soul, and forget not all his benefits-who forgives all your sins and heals all your diseases, who redeems your life from the pit and crowns you with love and compassion..."-Psalm 103:2-4, yet he was not healed. the anger that was welling up deep inside of his innmost parts, he laid bare before the throne of God. He was real with God about how he was feeling, and God responded. God likes it when his children contendend with him. He likes it when remind him of His promises. This concept of contending is all throughout the scriptures.

Jacob Contends

Jacob contended with God in Genesis 32:22-32. Jacob literally wrestled with God. Why? He realized who he was wrestling, and Jacob refused to give up, he refused to give in until God blessed him. God and Jacob wrestled all night. This was not a little Father/son wrestling match. Jacob was serious about receiving God's blessing. Jacob was desperate for it. He said, "I will not let you go until you bless me." At this statement of Jacob's God asked him, "What is your name?" "Jacob,"(which means Deceiver by the way). Then God Says, "Your name will no longer be Jacob, but "Israel" because you have struggled **with God and overcome." Jacob literally means —one who contends with God. We must learn to contend like Jacob did. We must learn to NOT give up.**

Abraham Contends

Abraham contended with God over Sodom and Gomorrah. He confronted God in Genesis 18:23-25," Will you sweep away the righteous with the wicked? ...will you really sweep it away and not spare the place
for the sake of the fifty righteous people in it? Far be it from you to do such a thing-to kill the righteous with the wicked, treating the righteous and the wicked alike. Far be it from you! Will not the Judge of all the earth do right?" Abraham was bold! He confronted God and held Him accountable to His goodness. He was contending for the righteous and confronting God knowing that God's character was at stake here. Abraham knew that God would NEVER destroy the righteous along with the wicked. He stood in the gap. He contended.

Stewarding Faith

I love the Wigglesworth quote at the beginning of the chapter. It is true. God loves to find faith on the earth. He is attracted to it and when He finds it He goes directly to it. As believers in Jesus Christ, we should be attracting God everywhere we go by our expectation of what we believe He will do. That is faith. It is faith that moves the hand of God. It is faith that manifests the impossible. Faith is contending and God loves it when we contend. We all have been given a measure of faith, however, we are each in charge of our faith level. We must steward our faith. We manage it. We can grow in it. We can activate our faith by stepping out and believing God, and God will prove Himself which will continue to increase our faith, or we can allow doubt to enter in which will diminish our faith. The very moment Peter stepped out of the boat he activated his faith. He believed that he could walk to Jesus on the water because He trusted Jesus that much. He EXPECTED to do it and he did. However, in a moment of doubt suddenly his faith waned, and he began to sink, but PETER WALKED ON WATER! Are you getting this?

Move the Spirit of God

God is attracted to faith. Faith literally moves the hand of God. When we believe God, and take Him at His Word, mountains are moved, cancer disappears, demons leave, etc. Smith Wigglesworth used to say, "if the Spirit isn't moving, then I'll move Him." Wigglesworth's unwavering belief in the Word of God and his expectation that God would show up was behind this bold statement. And guess what? God would show up. Wigglesworth was a contender! Heidi Baker, a modern day missionary to Mozambique says, "There is always enough." She expects there to always to be enough because she believes God, and He has never let her down. She and her husband, Rolland, with their ministry, Iris Ministries, serve in Mozambique. They serve thousands of orphans, and they have the privilege to feed and clothe them. These children have many needs. The Bakers and those in their ministry have experienced supernatural provision again and again. Why? Because they are contenders.

They expect it. God does not disappoint. They persist in seeking God and He keeps showing up. Heidi Baker contends for the orphans that have nothing, and God responds to her faith and the faith of others that cry out to Him on behalf of those children. Faith is expectation.

Abraham believed that God was going to supernaturally raise Isaac from the dead after God asked him to sacrifice his son. It was credited to him as righteousness because of his great faith. God asked him to do the unthinkable. He did not understand why God would ask him to sacrifice the very son God promised him, but because God asked him to do it he was willing to obey, believing God was going to do something supernatural to restore Isaac back to him-Hebrews 11:19. God did provide another sacrifice. He never wanted Abraham to sacrifice Isaac. God was testing Abraham's heart. God wanted to know if Abraham loved Isaac more than Him? Abraham's EXPECTED God do something supernatural. He did not know how God was going to do it, but he expected it. We need to be a people who expect God to do the miraculous. We must be persistent in knocking on the door of heaven. When we keep knocking on the door it demonstrates our expectation that God is going to answer. He wants to see how badly we want it. Do we really believe Him? How easy is it for us to give up? What are we setting our eyes on? Faith is the substance of things hoped for, the evidence of things not seen. That is how scripture defines faith. Faith is EXPECTATION, not just belief. Faith means, "I take God at His Word. He is not a man that He should lie - Numbers 23:19, therefore I EXPECT God to move in this situation." When God sees that kind of persistence and expectation in our hearts, He shows up! There is a difference between a belief in something and an expectation of something. If we want to see God move and do the miraculous, we must expect Him to move, and not just believe that He can.

When we read the New Testament, we see that Jesus was moved by faith so often. Faith moved Him. Those that contended for answers are the ones that received their miracle. When He saw faith in others, He could not help but be moved. Jesus teaches this concept to His disciples. Jesus told his disciples that if they had faith as small as a mustard seed they could tell a mountain to move from here to there and it would. He said "nothing will be impossible for you." Matthew 17:20.
He also told them if they had faith as small as a mustard seed, they could tell a mulberry bush to be uprooted and be planted into the sea, and it would obey. (Luke 17:6) Wow! Why do we miss these things in the Word of God? **Faith in Jesus can accomplish the impossible. We need Jesus to do the impossible in our own**

lives and in the lives of those we minister to.

Contending for the Miraculous

Let's look at some examples of New Testament contenders and how Jesus responded.

Mary's faith pulled the future into the present. Jesus' first miracle is documented in John 2: 1-11. This is where Jesus turns water into wine. Jesus was NOT the instigator of this miracle. It was His mother. She initiated it. Jesus told her to not involve Him because it was not yet His time. It was not time for Him to move into public ministry, but it was her faith that changed all of that. The faith of His mother brought what was to happen at a future time into the NOW. Jesus does NOT lie. He is perfect. He is sinless. So when He said, "it is not yet my time," then He meant exactly what He said, but the insistence of His mother telling the servants to do exactly what He said moved His heart. She had such great expectation that He could do something to help. All of a sudden, it WAS His time. Why is that? What changed? FAITH. Faith moved the hand of God. It is just as Wigglesworth said, "If God is not moving, then I will move Him." In this story, you have Jesus not moving, but Mary's persistence moved HIM! Her faith changed this entire situation. Her faith drew heaven to earth and heaven poured out the miraculous.

Nobleman Contends for His Son's Healing

In John 4:46-53 is the story of the nobleman who had faith in Jesus to heal his son. He begged Jesus to come down and heal his son. Jesus' response to the man seems odd. He said, "Unless you see signs and
wonders you will not believe." The nobleman did not even respond to Jesus'

statement. He could have. He could have chosen to be offended at what Jesus said, but instead of choosing offense, he chose to contend for the miraculous. He focused only on Jesus. He was not deterred. His faith and His persistence moved the heart of Jesus. After Jesus' statement he said, "Sir, come down before my child dies." Jesus said, "Your son will live." Jesus often offends our minds to get to our hearts. He
said what he said to challenge the faith of this royal official, however, the official did not take the bait. He expected Jesus to heal his son. He knew that Jesus could do it, and he contended! Jesus loves this kind of faith. It moves Him.

Friends Contend for Their Paralyzed Friend's Healing

Matthew 9:2-8; Mark 2:3-12, Luke 5:18-26

This is the story of the paralyzed man who was brought by his friends to a house where Jesus was teaching. The friends had such great expectation that they lowered him down through the roof because they could not get through the door to get him to Jesus because it was so crowded. This took a lot of effort on their part. First they had to carry him up to the roof, and then they had to dig out the roof so they could lower him down in front of Jesus. That certainly seems like a lot of trouble for them to go through doesn't it? His friends knew that if they could get their paralyzed friend to Jesus, he would be healed. And Jesus did not disappoint. The man was healed. Their actions demonstrated persistence. They expected their friend to be healed. They contended for his healing. What do you expect God to do? If we expect nothing we will get nothing, but if we expect the miraculous, then we will receive it.

Centurion Knew Jesus Could Heal with Just a Word

Luke Matthew 8:5-10

A Centurion comes to Jesus saying that his servant is sick and is suffering terribly. Jesus asks him, "Shall I come to him?" This was a challenge to the Centurion's faith. Jesus knew He did not have to physically be there to heal the man's servant. The centurion's response amazed Jesus. He basically said (My paraphrase), "I am a man of authority, and when I say to do something, my servants do it because I am in charge of them. You can just speak a word. There is no need for you to come." Jesus said that He had not seen faith such as this in all of Israel.

In Luke 7 it is written that the centurion's servant was healed. What can we learn from this story? One, the centurion came to Jesus knowing that Jesus had authority to heal. Two, He had enough faith that all Jesus had to do was speak a word and it would be done, and he expected Jesus to heal his servant. This man, who was a Roman soldier, understood Jesus' authority more than anyone in Israel did. He contended for his servant's healing. This man's faith moved Jesus!

Women with Issue of Blood Contends for her own Healing

Matthew 9:20-22; Mark 5:25-32; Luke 8:43

This is the story of the woman with the issue of blood. The Bible tells us that she had this issue for twelve years. The most important part of this story is that this woman, by Jewish Law, was not supposed to be in public. She was not supposed to be around other people because her condition made her "unclean." In Deuteronomy 15 when a woman has a discharge of blood for many days at a time other than her monthly period or has a discharge that continues beyond her period, she will be unclean as long as she has the discharge, just as in the days of her period. Any bed she lies on while her discharge continues will be unclean, as is her bed during her monthly period, and anything she sits on will be unclean, as during her period. Anyone who touches them will be unclean; they must wash their clothes and bathe with water, and they will be unclean till evening. She was supposed to be on the outskirts of the city, and she was not supposed to be around anyone else because by doing so, she would defile them and make them unclean. The traditions of the Pharisees watered down the Old Testament law, and changed it up some by saying that if an unclean person was to come near another they had to follow their procedure which was to identify themselves as "unclean."

The woman was supposed to yell, "unclean unclean," as she approached the crowd of people. She did not do that which put her as risk of being exiled or possibly even stoned to death. So, by the very fact that she approached Jesus in public demonstrates her persistence to contend for her own healing. The Bible tells us that she EXPECTED to be healed. She knew that if she only touched the hem of Jesus' garment, she would be healed. This was not going to be easy. There were crowds of people around Him. Many were bumping up against him and many reached out and touched him. This took great determination on her part. She pressed through the crowd probably touching many people while trying to get to Jesus, but all she was focused on was getting to him, getting close enough to just touch His clothes. She was probably really weak in her condition, but she pressed in and finally got close enough to touch the hem of Jesus' garment. As soon as she touched Jesus, He felt power leave Him.

This is a powerful principle right here. He literally felt power leave His body when this woman touched Him. Her faith drew out power from Jesus. There were many other people touching Him, too, but only this one he noticed. He could feel power leave Him. Please do not miss this point. Her expectation, her determination, and her persistence drew out power from Jesus. Jesus immediately stopped and wanted to know who touched Him. This woman had to be terrified because now she was going to have to be identified. She was going to be exposed as an "unclean" person, and everyone would know that she had violated the law and put other people at risk by being in such close proximity to them. After Jesus asked the question, she confessed that it was she who had touched Him. She was probably fearing the worst, but instead she heard Jesus declare, " your faith has healed you."(My paraphrase), "Daughter, your determination and persistence to come to me has healed you." Isn't this amazing?

This story has probably encouraged me more than any other. This nameless woman inspires me. Jesus' response to her melts my heart. He loves it when we pursue Him like that. What is holding us back?
Why aren't we contending for our miracle the way this woman did? All odds were against her. She had **no money because she spent it all on doctors who could do nothing for her. She was isolated and alone and labeled "unclean," but her desire to be healed drove her to Jesus. She knew if** she could just get to Jesus she would receive her healing. Expectation is everything. We will get what we expect.

Canaanite Woman Contends for Her Daughter's Healing

Matthew 15:21-28; Mark 7:25-30

Here is a story of a Gentile woman who comes to Jesus seeking healing for her daughter who was demon-possessed. She came to Jesus crying out for mercy. Jesus and His disciples made a 50 mile journey on foot for this encounter, but Jesus is the only one who knows the real mission. This woman is about to have an encounter with the Living God that will change her current reality.

Mark 7:25-30
In fact, as soon as she heard about him, a woman whose little daughter was possessed by an impure spirit came and fell at his feet. The woman was a Greek, born in Syrian Phoenicia. She begged Jesus to drive the demon out of her daughter. "First let the children eat all they want," he told her, "for it is not right to take the children's bread and toss it to the dogs." "Lord," she replied, "even the dogs under the table eat the children's crumbs." Then he told her, "For such a reply, you may go; the demon has left your daughter." She went home and found her child lying on the bed, and the demon gone."

Here you have a woman who, as soon as she heard about Jesus, came to Him and fell at his feet. The woman was not Jewish but Greek. She knows that He is the Messiah because she called him "Son of David", so she KNEW who He was. She begged Jesus to drive the demon out of her daughter. Jesus' response seems so harsh, but we must examine His motive for saying what He did. Jesus' initial reply was, "for it is not right to take the children's bread and toss it to the dogs," meaning "I came to the Jews first, and you are not Jewish, so I can't help you because of that."

Remember, Jesus would often offend the mind to get to the heart and that is exactly what He was doing here. How bad does she want her daughter to be healed? Will she walk away offended? This woman refused to allow that to get in her way and her response is absolutely amazing. She replied to Jesus, "even the dogs under the table eat the children's crumbs," or in other words, "Hey, I'll take whatever I can get. I just want some of what you have for my daughter." Her determination to pursue Jesus no matter what moved His heart. She contended for her miracle. "For such a reply, you may go." She had great faith! She did not give up! She contended for her daughter's deliverance. FAITH! EXPECTATION! She expected Jesus to heal her daughter. She expected Jesus to give her exactly what she was asking for. She was not leaving until she received what she came for. Her daughter was healed instantly. When she arrived home her daughter was back to normal.

Three Kinds of People

Remember, there are three kinds of people:

1. People who do not believe in miracles, and therefore they do not have any.
2. People who believe in them, but do not have them.
3. People who believe in them and have them.

What is the difference between the second and the third group? EXPECTATION! CONTENDING!

That is the difference. When we expect God to show up, He does. Our level of expectation exposes what is in our hearts. It exposes what we believe about Him. We can have head knowledge and read about all of the miracles, etc, and believe that He can do anything, but where is our expectation? That is what Jesus wants to know. What do you expect Him to do? If we expect Him to do nothing, then we will get nothing, but if we keep knocking on the door to heaven and we expect God to show up, then we will get exactly what we expect! Jesus' mother EXPECTED that He would do something miraculous at the wedding in Cana. She refused to take no for an answer, and so did the woman with the issue of blood, the Canaanite woman, and the Centurion. Keep knocking! Keep pursuing! Contend for your own miracle and for the miracles for others. God is looking for a place to land. Your faith is the runway!

CHAPTER 7: BE INSPIRED BY THE TESTIMONY

"In sharing testimonies and ministry our hearts should always be to draw people to the awe of Jesus and how amazing our heavenly father is."-Chris Gore -Founder of Kingdom Releaser Ministries

Testimony-evidence or proof provided by the existence or appearance of something; a public recounting of an experience.

God Wants to do it Again

The word for testimony comes from a Hebrew root word which means to do again. When we hear a testimony about something glorious God has done, it points to God's heart and it helps us understand that He did it once, and that He wants to do it again. Testimonies testify of God's character, and how amazing He is, but testimonies also stir the heart of the hearer. Testimonies create an environment for God to repeat what He has already done. Bill Johnson, of Bethel Church in Redding, California tells a story of a woman who was sitting in a church service who heard a story of a child getting healed of a club foot. As she sat in the service listening to the testimony of this young boy being healed of a club foot, she said to herself, "I'll take that for my daughter." Her child had feet that severely pointed inward. Her two year old daughter was in the nursery at the time. She heard a testimony of a boy being healed of a club foot, and she received it for her daughter. She grabbed hold of truth and claimed it. After the service, she went to the nursery to get her child, and discovered that her daughter was completely healed. That is the power of the testimony! Just as Chris Gore said in the opening quote, testimonies should always point to how amazing our Heavenly Father is. God is good. Knowing that God is good means that He wants to do it again. When someone recounts a testimony it stirs up hope in those that hear it. That is the point. Testimonies are very powerful. Where there was no hope, now all of sudden, after hearing of something great God has done, a shift happens in the thinking of those that thought they were facing an impossible situation. Hearing or reading testimonies remind us that Jesus can do the impossible. A seed is planted, and faith grows from this seed of hope. When we hear a testimony we should think, "If God can do that for them, then He can do that for me."

I have witnessed this in my life when it comes to praying for people. |I have read many books by contemporary Generals of the faith who see the miraculous every day. I have also read books of the Generals of the past, and how God used them. I read about these great men and women and their experiences all the while believing that God could use me the same way. I am crazy enough to think, "If God can use them then He can use me." Their testimonies inspire me to go after more. They are
ordinary men and women who were in love with Jesus and who wanted more of God, and had faith to believe God for the impossible. Because they believed, expected, and pursued, God did use them in the
impossible!

I said in the beginning of this book that I do not claim to be an expert. I only claim to be a follower of Jesus. What I am sharing with you, I have been going after myself, and I have seen a measure of breakthrough. I know more is coming. One thing that inspires me, besides Jesus Himself, is hearing the testimonies of others. When I hear the testimonies of how God has used someone to be a vessel to bring about a miracle for someone, my heart leaps inside of me because | understand that God wants to use me the same way. If He can use them, then He can use me.

Testimonies Build Faith

Sitting under the teaching of others and hearing their testimonies is a great faith builder. Earlier I shared that I attended a school of supernatural ministry.

During the ten months I attended the school, I sat under the teaching of great leaders who walk in the supernatural. I heard testimony after testimony. After graduation from SOM my heart was transformed. I was more inspired than ever to walk in the supernatural. I have been on a journey these past four years learning, growing, and pursuing more and more of God and what it means to walk in the supernatural. I left with a new confidence to lay hands on people and to see them healed. I began to understand that this was part of my call, and that I was to pursue God and His goodness and to exalt Him over every other standard. I began to preach healing in my church, teach classes on it, and I prayed for more people than I ever had before and I saw a measure of breakthrough. I was excited about every healing that I saw and was a part of. One in particular was a teenage boy named Robert that attended our church. He had some pain and some ringing in his ear one Sunday morning. He asked me to pray, so I did. I laid my hands on his ear and immediately, he felt a pop. The pain and ringing instantly stopped. Thank you Jesus! God is faithful!

Jesus Goes Viral

Testimonies encourage others and increase their faith! This is why crowds of people followed Jesus everywhere He went. They would experience a miracle and then tell others. Others course they wanted to experience what the other person experienced. They thought, "If Jesus can do it for them, then He will do it for me." So, before social media, Jesus went viral so to speak. Why? The **power of the testimony, that is why.**

Jesus Talks With a Samaritan Woman

John 4

Now Jesus learned that the Pharisees had heard that he was gaining and baptizing more disciples than John—although in fact it was not Jesus who baptized, but his disciples. So he left Judea and went back once more to Galilee.

"Now he had to go through Samaria. So he came to a town in Samaria called Sychar, near the plot of ground Jacob had given to his son Joseph. Jacob's well was there, and Jesus, tired as he was from the journey, sat down by the well. It was about noon. 7 When a Samaritan woman came to draw water, Jesus said to her,

"Will you give me a drink?" (His disciples had gone into the town to buy food.)

The Samaritan woman said to him, "You are a Jew and I am a Samaritan woman. How can you ask me for a drink?" (For Jews do not associate with Samaritan's.) 'Jesus answered her, "If you knew the gift of God and who it is that asks you for a drink, you would have asked him and he would have given you living water." "Sir," the woman said, "you have nothing to draw with and the well is deep. Where can you get this living water? "Are you greater than our father Jacob, who gave us the well and drank from it himself, as did also his sons and his livestock? "Jesus answered, "Everyone who drinks this water will be thirsty again, "but whoever drinks the water I give them will never thirst. Indeed, the water I give them will become in them a spring of water welling up to eternal life." The woman said to him, "Sir, give me this water so that I won't get thirsty and have to keep coming here to draw water."

He told her, "Go, call your husband and come back." "I have no husband," she replied. Jesus said to her, "You are right when you say you have no husband. "The fact is, you have had five husbands, and the man you now have is not your husband. What you have just said is quite true." "Sir," the woman said, "I can see that you are a prophet. Our ancestors worshiped on this mountain, but you Jews claim that the place where we must worship is in Jerusalem." "Woman," Jesus replied, "believe me, a time is coming when you will worship the Father neither on this mountain nor in Jerusalem.

He was not judging her nor was He condemning her for her many marriages or the fact that she was living with a man that was not her husband now. When Jesus told her personal things about her life, instead of being offended; this woman felt true love from Jesus. He was getting to the root of her issues. Men were not her answer. He was telling her that she needed more than just water from a well. She needed the Living Water that He offered. As Jesus spoke, she felt love and hope. How do I know that? Because of her response. This woman's life was changed because of one encounter with Jesus. She left the well and went back to her city and told everyone about this Jesus whom she had met that day. After hearing the testimony about her encounter with Jesus they had to come see for themselves. Many more became believers because of this woman's testimony! We cannot overlook the power of the testimony. They wanted to experience what she experienced, and see what Jesus did? He did it again, and "because of his words many more became believers." Isn't that amazing? The testimony of one woman was the catalyst that saved an entire city was saved.

My Personal Pursuit Drove Me

to Learn From Others

In my pursuit of more, I discovered a lady who had a world-wide healing ministry. I did not realize at the time that I heard about her that her ministry was located not too far from where live. I was intrigued by her ministry so I began reading her books and following her ministry. Amazing things happened when she prayed for people. People were miraculously healed. I was so inspired. I wanted what she had. I sat under her teaching, and learned all that I could from her. Every testimony I heard or read inspired me to want more. I attended her healing school, and became ordained under her ministry. Shortly after ordination, one night, I went to a healing service as part of her team, and at the end of the service I had an opportunity to pray for a boy who had some issues with his hip and leg. He did not have full range of motion, and he even walked with a slight limp. He was the pastor's son of the church where we were ministering. I prayed for the boy that night, and he was healed. He received full range of motion and was jumping around and playing. He was so excited to be able to move freely. His mother was very excited as well! That built my faith. Wow! God is so good. Another time, as I prayed as part of her prayer team at an event she was having I prayed for a woman who had an injured knee due to an ACL injury and meniscus injury. She could not move her knee or bend it. After I prayed, she received full range of motion and was even jumping on it. She was so excited and so was I. Thank you Jesus!

More Testimonies

Let's look at some amazing testimonies of God's working in the earth today. Allow these testimonies to spur you on! In Expecting Miracles: True Stories of God's Supernatural Power and How You Can Experience It, by Heidi and Rolland Baker, Rolland Baker tells a story of how his wife, Heidi prayed for a man in a village in Mozambique they visited. He was blind and lame. The man she prayed for was not healed right away. This did not discourage her. She asked them to send a runner to tell her when he was healed. I love her expectation that even though he did not get healed right away, she expected that he would be. The very next day she was visiting with a Muslim friend and businessmen when a runner ran up to the car she was in to tell her that the the man she had prayed for could now see and walk. The runner had run seven hours to give her this report. The people she was with obviously heard the report and because of the amazing testimony they wanted Heidi to pray for them. The power of the testimony moved the hearts of these men who were not followers of Jesus.

Randy Clark tells a story in Healing Unplugged: Conversations and Insights from Two Veteran Healing Leaders about a healing of woman from the Ukraine after

he received a word of knowledge. The word of
knowledge came to him in an unusual way, and it seemed like it was for someone in a rural area, and they were in a big city ministering, so he was hesitant to speak out the word. The word of knowledge came to him in a picture in his mind. In the picture he saw a blade from a big piece of farm equipment fall and cut off someone right at the knees and the damage was severe. He finally got the courage to speak out the word at the end of the service and a woman in the back raised her hand. She was in her sixties but was injured in the exact way he described when she was a teenager. She had not been able to walk normally and she could not even bend her knees. She had to walk up stairs backwards because of the extent of her injuries. She was instantly healed when he spoke the word and she responded. Isn't that amazing? That gets me very excited! God is so good. He met that woman right there in the Ukraine and used a man who was willing to speak out a word of knowledge, not knowing if anyone would respond.

This past year I prayed for a woman named Melody who was experiencing severe pain in her abdomen. She had suffered from gallstones, and was due to go back to the doctor that same week. I asked her if I could pray for her, and she said yes, so I did. I laid my hands on her and prayed a prayer believing that the stones would dissolve and that the doctors would find no evidence of the stones. I found out later that week that the report she received from the doctor was exactly that. There were
no stones, and the pain she was having was completely gone. To God be the glory!

God is so good. Another time I prayed for a lady named Cecilia who I went to church with. She was having **trouble with her left knee and she came to the altar to receive prayer. I laid my hand on her** knee and began to declare healing in Jesus' Name. She told me that as soon as I laid my hands on her knee, she felt like she had an Icy-Hot patch on her knee. She explained that it went from cold to really warm, and that the pain in her knee left. Thank you, Jesus! There was another lady that I attended church with named Haley. On several occasions, I prayed for her for different things and she was healed. One time, at a healing service we attended at another church, I laid my hands on her back and prayed for healing and her back was healed. Another time, Haley was began to have chest pains and was having trouble breathing, and as she describes it, a possible panic attack. I prayed with her and instantly she was healed. God is absolutely amazing!

What About the Ones that

do not get Healed?

I love testifying about God's greatness, and all that He has done, but the healings I do not see that drive me to keep knocking on the door of heaven and to keep contending and pursuing. I'll share one. This past year, while teaching a class on healing I knew of a lady in our community who was diagnosed with cancer. She had even attended one of our women's events the year before. At that women's event, I prayed for her at the church altar. I prayed my best prayer for her to be healed. She had a tumor in her stomach. I expected that tumor to dissolve, but unfortunately it did not. She came to church a few times afterwards, and then kind of fell off the radar. I then received a report from someone that she was dying. I received this news while I was teaching this class on healing. One Wednesday night, after everyone arrived, I told them we were going to take a field trip. I told them we were going to this lady's house to pray for her. I had called her earlier during the day to ask for permission to come to pray, and she said yes. The best way to learn is to go and do. We have to have the freedom to put into practice what we are learning. Just like Jesus created an atmosphere for His disciples to learn, we need that same grace. We need the freedom to learn. If I was teaching on healing, then this was a teachable moment for all of us. We can't let cancer scare us away. This lady desperately needed to be healed. So, me and about four other ladies drove to her house. She could not get up out of bed and she could barely talk. She was extremely weak, and it broke our hearts to see her in this condition. We were mad at the devil. So, we laid hands on her, prayed over her, declared over her, and even sang over her. We all prayed with great expectation. Unfortunately, we found out about a week or so later she passed away.

We Cannot Give Up

The enemy wanted to use this to take the wind out of our sails. We were all devastated that she lost her battle to cancer, but her death was another teachable moment. We cannot allow those that do not get healed to keep us from praying and seeking after God. Instead, we need to allow those to motivate us to **keep pressing in. The enemy wants to use the negative testimony to keep us from praying. He whispers, "Look what happened? You prayed and she died. See, God does not heal. You have no business praying for people. You are embarrassing yourself. You pray for people and they die." I have to confess that these thoughts entered my mind. But I made a choice to not stay there and to not entertain those lies. |began to cast down those vain imaginations. I let her death stir up more of a hunger in me.**

We have to get mad in the spirit and exalt the truth of the Word over what we do not see! We must keep pressing in, keep praying believing that God will show up! I hold on to the testimonies I've heard of those that have been healed of cancer, tumors dissolving, people driving thousands of miles to receive prayer and miraculously receive their healing. The testimony of those being healed of cancer inspires me to keep pressing in, to keep knocking, and to NOT give up. Every disease has to bow to the name of Jesus, and cancer must bow. But will we keep pursuing? Or will we give up?

Put Yourself in Places Where You Can Learn From Others

We cannot allow the enemy to discourage us. We need to build ourselves up in the faith and one of the ways we can do that is by allowing the testimony of others to encourage us. This is so important. How do we do that? We need to put ourselves in places where we can learn from others. Always seek God.

He is your number one source, of course, but it is okay to learn from others by going to conferences to learn more. Don't just be a conference junky! What does that mean, I'm sure you are asking? It is going from conference to conference without ever putting into practice what you are learning. Go! Learn! Do!

Another way we can learn from others in areas we want to grow in is by reading books by those who are walking in the supernatural. Allow their testimonies to move you and inspire you and motivate you to press in for more. I think it's also invaluable to learn from the healing leaders of the past and to glean from them as well. We can learn from the things they did right and we can learn from the things they did wrong. Some people refuse to learn from past leaders that have made mistakes. It's like they think the poor decisions of others will get on them. That is not true. If we are smart we will learn from the great things people have done, and we can learn from the mistakes that they have made. We learn from our own mistakes, so we can learn from the mistakes of others as well.

Books to Build Your Faith

I just want to share a few good reads with you. These are only suggestions, but I encourage you to read as much as you can from those that have walked in the supernatural and from those that currently walk in it today. There is much you can glean from others. Allow what God has done in the past to inspire you. Learn from the lives of others. The experiences of others is a feast for the one who is hungry.

Heidi and Rolland Baker — *Expecting Miracles: True Stories of God's Supernatural Power and How You Can Experience It*

Joan Hunter-*Healing Starts Now: Complete Training Manual*

Bill Johnson-*When Heaven Invades Earth: A Practical Guide to a Life of Miracles*

Bill Johnson and Randy Clark-*Healing Unplugged: Conversations and Insights from Two Veteran Healing Leaders*

Roberts Liardon-*God's Generals: Why They Succeeded and Why Some Failed*

CHAPTER 8: BE FILLED WITH THE SPIRIT

> *If through the Spirit, I spoke with tongues, then through the Spirit there could be other wonders. I have learned to live in the Spirit. I am on new ground where signs and wonders happen. Praise God - Reinhard Bonnke- Taking Action – Receiving and operating in the gifts and power of the HOLY SPIRIT*

The disciples obeyed Jesus and prayed for ten days after He ascended into heaven until The Day of Pentecost. It was on that day that they were baptized with power from Heaven. When you look at the word "power" from Acts 1 that Jesus used, it is the Greek word "dunamis," which Strong's defines as: strength power, ability, inherent power, power residing in a thing by virtue of its nature, or which a person or thing exerts and puts forth, power for performing miracles, moral power and excellence of soul.

In His eternal wisdom, Jesus knew His disciples would need this power and this ability to fulfill the Great Commission. If Jesus did not want His disciples to leave Jerusalem to try to win the lost without this power or this ability, then we should not attempt to do anything until we receive that same power. If the disciples needed to be filled, who walked with Jesus face to face, then so do we. We were given this gift. Jesus says it is a gift promised by His Father. You can choose not to accept the gift, but of course I don't recommend that. What we need to do is to receive the gift, open the gift, and wear this beautiful gift that was given to us because it equips us to replicate the Kingdom in the earth.

Dunamis Power

Here are some verses where the word "dunamis" is used.

Acts 1:8 "but you will receive power when the Holy Spirit has come upon you; and you shall be My witnesses both in Jerusalem, and in all Judea and Samaria and to the ends of the earth."

Acts 2:22 "Men of Israel, listen to these words: Jesus the Nazarene, a man attested to you by God with miracles and wonders and signs which God performed through Him in your midst, just as you yourselves know Samaria, and even to the remotest part of the earth."

Acts 3:12 "But when Peter saw this, he replied to the people, "Men of Israel, why are you amazed at this, or why do you gaze at us, as if by our own power or piety we had made him walk?"

Acts 4:7 "When they had placed them in the center, they began to Inquire, "By what power, or in what name, have you done this?"

Acts 4:33 "And with great power the apostles were giving testimony to the resurrection"

Acts 6:8 "And Stephen, full of grace and power, was performing great wonders and signs among the people of the Lord Jesus, and abundant grace was upon them all."

Acts 8:10 "and they all, from smallest to greatest, were giving attention to him, saying, "This man is what is called the Great Power of God."

Acts 8:13 "Even Simon himself believed; and after being baptized, he continued on with Philip, and as he observed signs and great miracles taking place, he was constantly amazed."

Acts 10:38 "You know of Jesus of Nazareth, how God anointed Him with the Holy Spirit and with power, and how He went about doing good and healing all who were oppressed by the devil, for God was with Him."

A Distinct Baptism

This power is available to every believer. Being baptized in the Holy Spirit equips us to accomplish all of the things that Jesus said we would do in John 14:12! It is essential to be the greater things generation. It is a separate infilling than that of being saved. Once we accept Jesus as our Savior, that means we are born-again into the Family of God, but being baptized with the Holy Spirit is an all-together separate experience. Some are under the impression that being born-again is the same thing as being baptized with the Holy Spirit. This is not true. When we become born-again, we all receive the Holy Spirit and He comes to dwell within the heart of every believer. We are the temple of the Holy Spirit. We have the honor to house the Holy Spirit, however, this gift of the baptism of the Holy Spirit is a distinct experience. Let's look at some verses in the Bible that illustrate this.

1. On the day of Pentecost in Acts 2 when "they were all together in one place," the pronoun "they" is referring to believers. Luke uses the Greek word "adelphon" which means brothers, meaning "brothers" in Christ. They had already put their trust in the resurrected Christ, and were obeying him. They were praying and waiting because He told them to. These people were already following Jesus. They were already saved, but on the Day of Pentecost "All of them were filled with the Holy Spirit and began to speak in other tongues as the Spirit enabled them." This was the first time the Spirit was poured out. It was on this day that the New Testament church was born. And how do we know that they were filled with the Spirit? They spoke in unknown tongues. They spoke in a language they had never learned. The evidence of the baptism in the Holy Spirit is speaking in tongues which can be heard. It manifested physically by them speaking in a language they never learned, and they could hear themselves and others speaking in these unknown tongues.

In all of the following examples you will see this. How did others know they were filled with the Spirit? Others could hear them speaking in tongues. This phrase "speaking in tongues" scares people. Here is all it means- speaking in a language you have never learned. We need to demystify speaking in tongues. It is Biblical. It is of God. It just means speaking in a language we have never learned. It is supernatural.

2. In Acts 8:14-16 it says, "When the Apostles in Jerusalem heard that Samaria had accepted the Word of God they sent Peter and John to them. When they arrived, they prayed for them that they might receive the Holy Spirit, because the Holy Spirit had not yet come upon any of them; they had simply been baptized

into the name of the Lord Jesus." Again this clearly shows that they had been saved. They had already received Jesus, "they had simply been baptized into the name of the Lord Jesus," but they had not received the baptism in the Holy Spirit. It says, "because the Holy Spirit had not yet come **upon any of them." This example is a clear distinction between being born-again, and being baptized in the Holy Spirit.**

3.In Paul's conversion in Acts 9 there is evidence that these are two separate experiences. After Paul's encounter with Jesus on the road to Damascus he immediately becomes obedient and does what Jesus tells him to do. "Now get up and go into the city, and you will be told what you must do." His traveling companions had to help him into the city because he was blind, but he did obey by demonstrating his submission to Christ. Then when Ananias arrives via the a instructions given to him in a vision, he calls Paul 'Brother" because knew Paul was now a believer in Jesus Christ. Believers in Jesus only addressed other born-again believers in this way by addressing them as "brothers."

Acts 9:17-19 says, "Then Ananias went to the house and entered it. Placing his hands on Saul, he said, "Brother Saul, the Lord Jesus, who appeared to you on the road as you were coming here-has sent me so that you may see again and be filled with the Holy Spirit." Immediately, something like scales fell from Saul's eyes, and he could see again. He got up and was baptized, and after taking some food, he regained his strength. So, in this example, Paul was saved after his encounter, but had not yet received the Holy Spirit. When Ananias places his hands on Saul to pray for him, the scales fell off of his eyes, and he received the Holy Spirit.

4. Acts 19:1-7 While Apollos was at Corinth, Paul took the road through the interior and arrived at Ephesus. There he found some disciples and asked them, "Did you receive the Holy Spirit when you believed?" They answered, "No, we have not even heard that there is a Holy Spirit." The very fact that Paul asked this question demonstrates two separate occurrences. He was asking, "Did you receive the Spirit's power when you believed?" If it was the same thing, then Paul never would have asked the question because it was his experience to come into contact with those who had accepted Jesus, but had not yet received the baptism in the Holy Spirit. He wanted to make sure that everyone he met had been baptized with Holy Spirit. If they were not, he wanted to lay on hands on them that they might receive it.

5. We cannot forget that when Jesus promises this gift of the Holy Spirit He only promises it to disciples in Luke 24 and in Acts 1. He does not promise it to those who need to be saved. He promises the Holy Spirit to those that already

follow Him. Luke 24:48-49 says, "You are witnesses of these things. I am going to send you what my Father has promised; but stay in the city until you have been clothed with power from on high." Acts 1:4-5 says, "On one occasion, while he was eating with them, he gave them this command: "Do not leave Jerusalem, but wait for the gift my Father promised, which you have heard me speak about. For John baptized with water, but in a few days you will be baptized with the Holy Spirit." Jesus gave this promise to those that were already following Him. This was not a promise for unbelievers, but for those who were born-again believers. All of these verses clearly show that being baptized in the name of Jesus (water baptism), believing in

Him and becoming a follower of Jesus is different than being baptized in the Holy Spirit. As Christians we need all that Jesus has to offer so as His Body, His Church, we can be fully equipped to do the Kingdom work He has called us to. We need the POWER He freely offers. Continually be Filled with the Spirit **Being baptized in the Holy Spirit is not a one-time event. It is not something we receive one time and then we are set for the rest of our Christian walk. No, it is a lifestyle that we should maintain. We need to continually be filled with the Holy Spirit as Paul says in Ephesians 5:18, "Do not get drunk on wine, which leads to debauchery. Instead, be filled with the Holy Spirit." What it really means in the Greek is "continually" be filled with the Spirit. It means that it should be a part of the** daily life of believers. It should be something that we continually do.

Also Paul says in 1Corinthians 14... "thank God that I speak in tongues more than all of you..." Paul is saying that he practices this "speaking in tongues" all the time. He even says that he does it more than they, the Corinthian Church, which shows that there are levels of this. Speaking in tongues is something that we steward just like we steward our finances, our faith, and our gifts. We must also steward speaking in tongues. It is something that we can grow in because if we don't, then we dry up and lose passion and power. It is vital that as the "called out ones" that we are equipped with every weapon possible to take on the enemy. A soldier would not go into battle without the proper weapons. His commanding officer would never dream of sending his soldiers into the field without proper training and weapons. When a man or a woman chooses to be in the armed forces, they go and sign up. They sign on the dotted line and then they are sent to boot camp for training. There, at boot camp they learn everything they need to know to be successful in battle, and it is then, after they are properly trained, that they are sent off to war. They are sent with all of the equipment and weapons they need to be successful in war. This is like the believer who chooses Jesus and they become saved. They immediately become part of the Lord's army. They have signed on the dotted line, but they still need more. As soldiers in the Lord's army we need all the equipment and weapons that He has provided for us. The baptism in the Holy Spirit is essential as we battle the enemy. The baptism of the Holy Spirit are our explosives given to us by our Commander. It is dunamis power! We need this explosive power! It never runs out! It is always available.

If we are serious about serving our Lord and bringing a demonstration of the gospel, rather than only an explanation of the gospel, then it is vital that we do not go into battle without being baptized in the Holy Spirit.

How to Receive the Holy Spirit

Many people are under the impression that you have to be at a church at the altar with someone laying hands on you to receive the Holy Spirit, but that is not true. A person can receive the Holy Spirit in many different ways. There is no ONE way to receive the baptism in the Holy Spirit. Personally, I was a Christian for almost three years before I was baptized with the Holy Spirit. I was 29 years old. I had a lot of preconceived ideas of what I thought being baptized in the Spirit was even after I became a Christian which made me fearful of it because

I did not understand it in my early walk with Christ. However, after a lot of prayer and pursuing God and reading the Word, I began to understand that it was Biblical and I wanted all that God had for me. I was at a women's retreat when I received the baptism. I was at my seat, standing up worshiping the Lord when I was filled. No one prayed for me. No one laid hands on me. I just asked the Lord to fill me, and I was open to receiving, and He filled me. I began to speak in other tongues. I had been seeking it for quite some time, but on that day at the women's retreat, in a room filled with hundreds other women, I was filled.

That's just my personal experience. A former pastor of mine received the baptism of the Holy Spirit when he was camping as a teenager. He was in a tent alone, praying and seeking God when he received the baptism. My oldest daughter received the baptism of the Holy Spirit when she was only eight years old. I have seen even younger children than that receive the baptism. God is amazing. If we seek Him, and we want all He has, He will give us what we ask for. There is no right way. Many people receive the baptism when they come to the altar to receive prayer. I have prayed for many to receive the baptism with the laying on of hands. I laid my hands on them, asked the Lord to pour out His Spirit on them, and they received. Many receive the Spirit in this way. Others may be at home seeking God and asking Him to fill them. A friend of mine was in her room praying and seeking God and as she says, "it came gushing out." My daughter reminded me of a story that I had forgotten about. When she was around nine years old, she and another girl that we attended church with who was eight years old laid hands on a woman at the instruction of the Pastor, to receive the baptism in the Holy Spirit, and the woman was filled. Isn't that awesome? The Pastor knew that the two young girls had been filled with the Spirit and these two children laid hands on an adult, and she was filled! There is no Jr. Holy Spirit. God will use whoever is willing. Being filled with the spirit is vital to walking in POWER!

Why would't we want all that God has? I want every bit that He offers. I want to walk in the fullness of the power. If He says I need to to walk in that power, then I want it. I want you to have it too. It will change you. If want the infilling of the Holy Spirit, seek God. Ask Him. He wants to fill you, and He will. How will you know when you have been filled? You will speak in a language you have never learned. You won't know what you are saying, but your spirit will, and your spirit will be communing with God. I pray that the verses I have provided for you are helpful in leading you to see that this is Biblical, and why you need it.

CONCLUSION

If you are believer in Jesus, then you are qualified to walk in the supernatural. That is all there is to it. There are no other qualifications. So, how come more believers are not seeing these signs wonders, and miracles that we read about in the Bible? We have been passive. We have misunderstood what our goal is as followers of Jesus.

I hope you have been challenged to not allow the theology, doctrine, opinions, or the persuasion of others to deter you from your quest of going after all that God has purchased for His children. If He died to give it to you, then it is worth having. There are levels of revelation, and He has more for those who will seek more. I want you to be a part of God's vast army.

I want to encourage you to pursue God. Go after Him. Go after what Jesus has promised us. He wants to use you. He just wants your heart and He wants you sold out for Him. Who is this greater things generation Jesus spoke about in the New Testament? It is YOU! You are this generation. You are about to be a part of the greatest outpouring of the Holy Spirit the world has ever seen. This book is an attempt to encourage and inspire those looking for more in their walk with Jesus. Our calling is not to just be "saved" and wait to go to heaven. Our calling is so much more. We get to partner with the One who created us, and He wants us to use each of us to build His Kingdom, right here on earth.

Remember, walking in the supernatural is not just for the ones with a title, or the ones who speak behind the pulpits, or the ones with fancy theological degrees. No! This is for the one who desires more! The one who has had an encounter with the Living God and wants to lead others into their own encounter.

Pursue intimacy, quit making excuses, lay down your preconceived ideas and doctrines, understand that Jesus is willing, understand that you have authority to command and make declarations, be a contender, be inspired by the testimony, and be filled with the spirit! If you are hungry and you aren't sure where to start, these are some steps that you can follow to help you. God is waiting for you. He died for you. He loves you. He wants your heart, and He wants to use you to build His Kingdom. I challenge you! Transform yourself into the greater things generation, and your life will never be the same and you will play a crucial role in building God's Kingdom! You will have a part in populating heaven.

John 14:12 "And you will do even greater things than these." Be inspired! I hope this book has helped you see that this is you. YOU are the Greater Things Generation!

Made in the USA
Columbia, SC
27 April 2020